the austin student anthology

NOTABLE FICTION AND ESSAYS 2010

This book is a collection of works of fiction and essays. Names, characters, businesses, organizations, places, events, and incidents are either a product of the authors' imagination or are used fictitiously. Any resemblance to actual persons, living or dead, events, or locales is entirely coincidental.

Published by Legacy Book Company
Austin, TX
www.legacybookcompany.com

For ordering information or special discounts for bulk purchases, please contact Legacy Book Company at PO Box 91869, Austin, TX 78709, 512.891.6100.

Design and composition by Greenleaf Book Group LLC
Cover design by Greenleaf Book Group LLC
Project Manager: Chris McRay, Greenleaf Book Group LLC

ISBN 13: 978-0-9841892-3-6

Part of the Tree Neutral® program, which offsets the number of trees consumed in the production and printing of this book by taking proactive steps, such as planting trees in direct proportion to the number of trees used: www.treeneutral.com

Printed in the United States of America on acid-free paper

10 11 12 13 14 15 10 9 8 7 6 5 4 3 2 1

First Edition

contents

introduction

GREENLEAF BOOK GROUP IS PROUD TO introduce the *Austin Student Anthology*, a collection of short stories written by some of the most talented young authors in Austin, Texas.

As a top publisher and distributor for independent authors and small presses, Greenleaf Book Group has long been committed to developing the art of writing among young and old alike. With this mission in mind, we launched the Big Bad Story Contest in the spring of 2010. Our intention in running the contest was to give exceptional local students the opportunity to become published authors, a distinction that will help open doors as they make their way on life's journey.

More than seventy students from four schools entered

the contest. The chosen thirteen appear in this anthology. We wish to thank the participating schools and dedicated teachers and parents who supported these students in their efforts. Especially, thanks to Jason Farr, NBCT, of Anderson High School, Dan Reynolds of San Juan Diego Catholic High School, Annie Mikesell of Premier High School of North Austin, and Loren Schauer and Elizabeth D. Camarena of Premier High School–South.

As varied in style as the students who produced them, these stories offer memorable insights into the turbulent and challenging world of today's high school students. The talent of these students, and the dedication of their teachers, is evident throughout the book. Each of the authors included in this anthology (as well as their teachers and parents) should take pride in their talent, their commitment, and their hard work. If, as so many claim, effective communication is the key to success, all of these authors should expect a bright future in their chosen field of endeavor.

Congratulations, authors, and never stop writing.

Greenleaf Book Group

bears and men on a watercolor day

madeline vuong

GRAMPS IS REALLY GREAT. EVERYONE respects him 'cause he was in the military and you can just tell he's no wuss. After any boy in my family turns eleven, they get to go out for a week to Gramps's hunting lodge in the Pine Barrens for their "glory kill." The glory kill is like one of those Indian spirit-vision quests, except when you see *your* animal, instead of naming yourself after it, you kill it. Gramps took my cousin Roy out two years ago, and they shot this great big buck. Its head is mounted above the mantel in the lodge. Everyone treated Roy differently after he came back because that buck proved he was a man. I know I'm going to get something even better for *my* kill because it's open season on the black bears in the Barrens.

My name is Jake—I just turned eleven last week, and this is *my* year to kill a bear. I can just feel it. Gramps is going to show me how to be a man, and everyone will remember the day I become transformed when my roaring bear head replaces Roy's piddly buck over the mantel. Man, will Roy be jealous!

I'm thinking about my glory kill as I go inside the lodge. For a few seconds after I enter, it's hard to make out much else besides Roy's buck because only the reflective glass eyes Gramps installed in the empty sockets in the skull shine out from the gloom.

A voice barks from the shadows behind me, "Be alert! Always be alert, Jacob. The bears won't wait for you to think. They won't play nice."

I turn around and try to look like I'm not startled at all, which is hard since all the hairs on my arms are sticking up, all freaked out like, giving me away.

Gramps gives me a manly clap on the back in greeting. "Hello, son. Just gotta wait for your grandmother to finish making us some food and we'll go." He exhales irritably, "Where *is* that damned woman?"

Gramps yells for Gran, who comes in from the kitchen dressed in a frilly white apron. "What?" she asks.

"Don't you 'what' me in that tone, woman," Gramps barks, and Gran immediately lowers her gaze.

"Sorry, Erv."

"Stop wasting my time and pack us some sandwiches. We could've been headed out by now," Gramps growls.

Gran looks like she wants to come over to hug me, so I move strategically out of the way. Hugging is not manly, and today is all about finding out the secret from Gramps of what makes a boy turn into a man. Nothing can mess today up. I won't let it. Gran apparently takes the hint 'cause she vanishes back into the kitchen to get the sandwiches.

When Gran comes back in, Gramps checks inside one of the sandwiches, sloppily slapping the slices of bread back together in dissatisfaction. "Jesus, how many times do I have to tell you that I don't like the cheese?" His voice sounds like he's kidding but something hard in his eyes makes me think he's not.

"Those aren't yours," Gran tries to explain. "That's why they have cheese. Yours are just meat and tomato."

"Ugh!" Gramps exclaims. "How am I supposed to know that when you don't label them? And these feel too light. Not enough meat." He picks up a sandwich and shakes it carelessly about so that the contents fall out into a pile of tomato gore and meat, spattering down onto the rest of the sandwiches on the plate. "I've never heard of anyone eating a *bread on bread* sandwich, have you?" He shakes the now empty sandwich around a little more to emphasize. "This is how a man handles a woman, Jacob," he tells me. He laughs at his own joke, so I laugh too, even though I'm not sure I know why it's that funny.

"Sorry, Erv," Gran says and picks up the sandwiches. As she turns to go, I notice something funny, something pinched about her expression, like she's accidentally taken a sip of lemonade before adding any sugar, but she doesn't look as surprised as you'd expect someone to be if they'd done that. It's like she knew it was just lemon juice but took a swig anyway. Before I can think too much on it though, she's disappearing back into the kitchen. Gramps leans back in his chair and winks at me.

I don't know why, but now I feel a little unsettled. Must be the nerves. I shove any possible uncertainty out of my mind and try to refocus. This is too important a day to be off my game. I wink bravely back at Gramps and wait for the sandwiches to come back.

After we have our sandwiches, Gramps lets me pick what gun I want to take out. I pick the 30.06. It's a classic but solid gun. I've got it in tight against my shoulder, pressing down into my collarbone. I can smell the oiled wood and this clinging smoky smell. It smells raw, like power—a whiff of my future. It smells like finally becoming a man. I am eleven. This is my bear hunt. I am ready to kill.

As we set out along the path into the thick of the Barrens, the sky is cloudless and a pure, piercing blue; it's the perfect day. The sky is so bright; it almost seems to bleed into the corners of my vision, mixing with the green trees and the brown of the dry leaves on the path like a watercolor: blue, green, brown. All the colors swirl in my stomach with my excitement.

Gramps says he saw fresh bear tracks down by Roscoe Stream the day before yesterday, so that's the direction we set out in. We hike an hour out into the tangled brush towards Roscoe Stream before we see torn branches, evidence that something has passed through. I see the tracks almost immediately after. They're absolutely massive, and suddenly I'm not sure that I can get a bear with just the 30.06. I'm wishing I'd taken out the .510, or something a little heftier. I'm not scared or anything, just a little, you know, concerned.

"These are new. From this morning, probably. He's only a few hours off," Gramps informs me, interrupting my thoughts. He's leaning up from the track with his whole body straining forward like a lean, gristly wolf. "If we hurry, we could catch 'im before nightfall up at the Point."

Gramps doesn't really like to talk. Thinks it's a waste of good airspace if you haven't got something important to say, so mostly I'm just hearing the crunch, crunch of our feet on leaves. We both know what we're here to do. We're tramping along and the hours all sound the same. Crunch, crunch. The sound is consistent and in your ears like a heartbeat. I wonder if this is what it's like to be in the military, having this rhythm that everybody shares. Maybe this is manhood, this shared tramping, over and over. We're like one person marching. I don't want to say anything to screw it up, so I keep my trap closed and keep walking, matching my footfalls to Gramps's, trying to copy every turn of his head, trying to avoid every leaf he avoids. I don't even look up because I'm afraid I'll break the spell of the march. Head down. Crunch, crunch. One heart. Crunch, crunch. One man.

Gramps's prediction is spot on. We track the bear all the way up to the Point, the highest part of the Barrens. We finally catch sight of him. He's huge and his fur sticks up all funny, making his outline look fuzzy, like a far-off, dark storm cloud.

"Alrighty, Jacob," Gramps tells me. "A little closer and you pop 'im like a virgin cherry." The sinews in his arm stick out as he makes his hand into a fist and crushes it against his other hand, illustrating what I'm to do to the bear.

I edge closer to him, taking care not to crack any dry sticks under my sneakers. The 30.06 is heavy in my grasp and I can feel my hand getting sweaty and nervous, sliding along the barrel as I creep along, closer and closer. I re-grip and my breath comes out shaky. My finger is slippery on the trigger. One shot. One shot to get the bear. One shot to get a bigger kill than Roy. One shot to prove myself to everyone. One shot to be a man.

I take careful aim at the blurry, dark shape in the distance, trying to line up the barrel of the gun in the straight line I'd practiced forever with my BB gun at home. Then, my heart thrumming in my chest, I pull the trigger. The shock almost knocks me over. It's partly the backfire of the gun, because it's a strong one, but it's more that I'm just not expecting the sound. It seems much louder than it should, like dropping a massive silver platter on the wood floor of a totally silent house. The sky is still blue, the leaves still green, the paths still brown, and suddenly I'm wondering if I've just imagined shooting the gun. There's this pause like the whole world is inhaling and holding its breath along with me, and nothing moves except my heart, which pumps blood everywhere at quadruple speed.

I almost pull the trigger a second time when I hear a wail, inhuman and shrill, and I know I've done it after all.

I've shot the bear.

But something's wrong. It's still running.

Black shadow and red and green are all running together. Bear, forest, and this red stuff. Red, all over. I'm running toward the bear and this red stuff; it's everywhere, everywhere. So red. It's blood. As soon as

I realize it, I can't get it out of my head. It smells sweet and hot and metallic and it's in my head and in my lungs and in my soul.

The bear falters, stumbles far up ahead, and, with a crash, it's down on its side. Panting, struggling to get back up. Drags itself a few feet. Oozing. Oozing red. I approach warily. I can hear Gramps behind me. The bear is keeled over. I can't stop looking. Finally, my eyes obey me and shut, but I can see the red blood vessels inside my lids. Red. It's everywhere. Red. It's all over the bear's fur, on the forest litter, staining my skin, even though I'm not touching it. This is the kind of blood you can't just wash off. You don't brag about this kind of blood. No, this kind of blood you keep quiet about.

"Shoot it," Gramps grunts from behind me.

I'm looking and everything is fuzzy like the bear's fur, and suddenly it's emitting that horrible wail again. I stand transfixed, looking at the bear. I can't move.

"Shoot it. C'mon Jacob, man up and finish the job." Gramps is impatient, angry at my hesitation. I'm paralyzed though. I try to stumble away from the mess of blood and leaves and mud that's everywhere, but my legs don't know me, and they don't move right. I waver.

Then, a shot shatters through my ears, jarring my bones, and the bear stops moving. More red. My hands are guilty, for I have killed. My fingers made me into a killer. I stare at them, stupefied. I didn't think it would be like this. I don't think I want to be a man anymore.

Gramps goes on about not half-assing kills while we get the bear together to be carried back. But the bear's dead, and Gramps is actually pretty satisfied, so we're back to silence fast. As I said before, Gramps doesn't like wasting breath when there's nothing to be said. The walk home is real quiet, too. Quieter without the squelch of knife in entrails. At least when we were preparing the bear, there was something to put in my mind, but now it's empty. There's too much unoccupied space and my thoughts echo around and my ears ring with it all. I feel like I want to say something, ask if this heaviness is right, if it's manly, but my whole body is numb from the shot—like the noise of it took all the noise inside me and only left this echoing emptiness. We walk mostly in silence, but our footfalls don't line up properly and we don't sound like one beating heart, but like desperate, arhymthical panting.

Gramps makes me help him drag the body. It still feels

warm and it reeks of sweet death. The fur touches my cheek as I drag the bear and I realize that it must be a baby, because no way we could drag a full grown one of these. It won't ever live to have an eleventh birthday. I want to tell Gramps it was wrong to kill it, that it was just a kid, but I can't because before I can open my mouth, my voice is already just echoes in my head. I keep dragging. I feel disgusted. I only look back once and the entire forest path is smeared red in our bloody wake. Thankfully, night falls quickly, covering up the evidence of my shame with darkness.

When we get back to the lodge, Gran comes out to see us drag in the bear. I keep my distance from her, but when Gramps goes in, I let her put her arms around me and I lean against her as she brushes the hair off my forehead. I close my eyes and finally it's dark behind my eyes and quiet in my head.

Gramps promises that my bear head will be up over the mantle next time I go to the lodge. I don't want to see it. The thought turns my stomach and I want to wretch out the sandwiches we ate that afternoon. Want to wretch out all the red tomato guts, to get them out of me. But I don't because Gramps is still watching me. Still talking.

"Your very own glory kill," he's saying. The victory feels like those fake glass eyes, just a shiny gloss over an empty socket in a skull.

• • • • •

When I see Cousin Roy the next day, he's definitely jealous because he completely ignores me, pretending to be absorbed in painting a picture. I should be rubbing my glory kill in his face, but I don't really have anything to say anymore. I look over at Roy's painting. He's a crap artist. He's used too much water, so blue and green and brown blur together, and suddenly the bear is staring out at me. Before I can stop them, my hands have reached over and smeared his picture so everything runs together and nothing is distinguishable anymore. Roy looks up in surprise and I'm looking at my hands all covered in blue and green and brown and, oddly, red.

"I . . . I'm sorry. I didn't know that would happen. I didn't mean to," I say.

I mean it to both of them.

save yourselves

rey acosta

[START OF RECORDING]

To whom it may concern,

My people are in danger. I will provide a little background first. My people are descendants from the survivors of the global destruction of Earth, December 21, 2012. We live on planet Gliese 581d. Our descendants left Earth once week before its destruction. Our founding father, known only as the Great Bin, still rules our nation after 300 years.

My life was perfect. Our lives were perfect. We lived in harmony. I couldn't imagine a life like the one my ancestors once had. Our lives could not be easier. Everything was planned out for us as birth. I was lucky enough to be chosen as the Great Bin's security guard. It was an easy job though. All I did was make sure no one went in or out of his quarters. He ran the whole nation from his living space. Only one person could go into his area and that was his political advisor, the Fair Kim. He was short and chubby. I believed he was on a special life-supporting drug because he had been the Great Bin's advisor since the Landing of our people 300 years ago.

The Great Bin had gone to great lengths to protect our people. He made it possible for everyone to have healthcare. His kindness was shown by the monitoring system we had. He watched our every move. He created many jobs including those of construction for our people. The people built shrines and statues of the Great Bin in his honor. Every citizen was satisfied with life. Violence was not a problem either but one thing had been worrying me. There had been disappearances that no one else had been noticing but me.

This is what happened:

It was just an ordinary day. Everything was running smoothly. Nothing was out of routine. The Fair Kim made it to his daily meeting with the Great Bin around noon. He was holding a big duffle bag like always. I had no idea the reason for it though. I sensed something different that day. The Fair Kim squeaked after every step. The next day he came back at noon for his meeting again. He wasn't squeaky this time. I thought to myself, "Hmm, that's odd." I left it at that. On month later he arrived squeaky again. I asked him, jokingly, "Feeling a little rusty in the joints today?"

"It is not a time to joke sir," he replied in a serious tone.

"Yes sir, carry on, sir."

He went inside the Great Bin's quarters. I heard loud, nervous yelling. It worried me. I figured something was wrong. The Fair Kim walked out. "What was that all about? Are we in danger?" I questioned.

"None of your business! Get back to work!" Kim snapped.

I felt disrespected. For the first time ever, someone infuriated me. The feeling was alien to me. Something took over me, "If you don't tell me then I will tell our people that something is not right!"

"Nothing is in danger. Besides no one would believe

you if there were," Kim rebuked while glaring at me with fierce red pulsing eyes.

I had never seen that before. I then knew something was really wrong. "Tell me what is wrong this instant or so help me I will—"

"You will what? Kill me? Not Possible!" he shouted as he interrupted.

"Wait what?!"

"You do not get it? I'm not human."

"What are you? What have you done with the Great Bin?"

"I do not have permission to discuss this subject any further."

The Fair Kim turned around to depart. A rage had taken over me before he could take two steps. I charged him and tried to tackle him. My head hit his rock-hard abs and I was knocked out.

I awoke while being dragged into the quarters of the Great Bin. Someone, something, greeted me, "Hello young rebel."

"Who are you?!" I shouted. My eyes were still adjusting to the lighting in the room.

"The Great Bin," it replied.

My sight returned to normal. "No you're not! You're . . . you're . . . you're a computer."

"Technically, no."

"What? What about the Fair Kim?"

"The Fair Kim is an android."

"What do you want to do with us?"

"Well, we are refugee alien slaves from another galaxy."

"And?"

"250 years ago we landed on this planet. The original Great Bin and Fair Kim attacked us. We killed them and my friend and I took their place as your people's leaders."

"Okay anything else?"

"Well, do you know about the disappearances?"

"Yes, I do, what about them?"

"We have found your people to be quite delectable."

"You're eating us?!"

"Yes. Now that you know, you're dinner!"

I took a run for it. The Fair Kim's android was chasing me. I told my friends what happened. I also told them to spread the word. My people are most likely enslaved or dead by the time you have finished listening to this. I have found a place to hide for now. I have made this tape to inform you to leave this planet the moment you no longer hear my voice. One more thing, the aliens control the android and super computer from the top floor of the Great Bin's quarters. If you have the guts, kill them and be successful or you might be breakfast. The android just passed by, he has said something about initiating some sort of farm. The farm will involve breeding my people for them to feed on. I think he just heard me . . .

[End of recording]

orpheus

samuel chapman

ASCETICS CAN'T BRING THEMSELVES TO disbelieve superstition. Luke knew he was wrong, but he couldn't help himself believing that all the skill would leave his fingers if he gave any serious thought to what he was doing. At the best of times he imagined an angel inside him, guiding him across the strings; at the worst—and there was no shortage of hard times for a troubador—he was a puppet with no strings, a prisoner of his art.

Chords were nothing, strumming was something more and less than robotic. Luke's instrument was his mind and he called himself a monk because he could only play when it was clear.

Today, there was something in the way. His pick caught at a crucial moment and he groaned in frustration. Except for his guitar, there wasn't a single ambient sound on the ridge. He was lying in the grass, in the early evening, before a folded valley shrouded with mist. If he couldn't play here, where the hell could he?

He slumped backward, letting his guitar slide through his hand and come to rest beside him. Maybe it was the fog.

"Damn fool," he heard the valley tell him. "Ain't nobody brings a guitar to the Blue Ridge. That's banjo country and you'd know if you'd thought two seconds about this whole damn game."

"Shut it," he replied to nobody. Luke shook his head to clear it. Christopher McKinney was nowhere for three states; for all Luke knew, his father had finally succumbed to scotch and slow living. He certainly wouldn't have cut a refrain short for the news.

Luke grasped the guitar by the base of the neck and pulled it upright, along with himself. He mulled the prospect of searching for a town for the night, wondering if he would be able to see one from his aerie once the mist cleared. What I'd really like to find, he thought, is a peasant village. All the houses built in a circle around a square with a roaring fire, where they'd be feasting and singing and inviting me to serenade them. Flowing ale, loose women. Maybe one of the hills was a fortress against time.

Now that the music had gone, Luke's pain returned. Hunger was beginning to eat away at him, gnawing around the edges of all his other thoughts, even ones it had no business being in. Walking usually chased it away, so Luke set off. There was only one path that led away from the ridge; shrouded by trees, it would lead him into the sheltered valley where he'd look for civilization.

He tried to distract himself as he entered the forest but couldn't think of anything to think about except the long distance through the valley ahead of him. Whenever he managed to push dread away, he settled on his father's scowl instead. Though he was almost afraid to do it, he came to rest at the only music that had defeated him time and time again: the opening chords—A minor, C major, G major, the first three he'd ever learned—of his anthem for Mary.

The prelude, and nothing more, had moved into his head the moment he'd first laid eyes on her, years ago when they were both seventeen. He'd been strumming on his porch in Appomattox; she'd been walking by and it had simply stopped her in her tracks. She'd fumbled to drop a backpack, and Luke recalled thinking how unfair it was that somebody that beautiful had also been gifted with functioning limbs. There had to be some kind of sacrifice made—but the closer they got, the more Luke knew there wasn't one at all. He accounted for the fatal flaws, the tragic *hamartia*, in their relationship.

Her Orpheus, she'd always called him. "Would you walk into the underworld to save me?" she'd asked one day.

"How did Orpheus handle it?" he replied.

"He had a lyre, a Thracian lyre," Mary explained. "He found his wife's soul in the gloom and led her out by playing. She just followed the music."

"Doesn't this story have a sad ending?"

"Who cares?" she laughed. "We write our own endings, right, Luke?"

That was what Luke had wanted when he set off. He was a musician through and through, but also a bit of a writer. Luke McKinney wanted to the author of his own endings, and his own beginnings and middles.

A sound echoed from the brush and Luke, always on guard now, fixated on the rustling that revealed the source of the noise. His drive for illogic, heightened by the mist, began looting the shelves of folklore to determine what his new company was. A headless prospector, or some hidden tribe forgotten by time. He decided on a dragon, and started to pray in his own way, shouldering his guitar and plucking a tentative arpeggio.

At that point, Luke became the first man in history to be relieved by the sight of a mountain lion. They were the one aspect of Appalachian existence he had found out everything about—he knew how cougars and pumas were different names for the same thing; what activities drew them; exactly how to scare them away. Terror could be the most effective teacher.

The animal didn't take interest in him at first. Luke tensed, unwilling to move. Running would be suicide. Darting his eyes around his body, he tried to note the exact position of every wavering muscle. The mountain lion was sniffing the ground, pawing its way along the rock face looming a few meters above the trail and looking disturbingly like a housecat.

Luke began to edge his arms toward the flaps of his jacket, wincing every time he made too sudden a move.

The cat glanced up and away again.

Luke clutched his jacket tightly, waiting for the right moment.

When the cat snarled in acknowledgment of new prey, Luke seized his chance and threw his coat open wide. With the sun at his back, he knew his entire body was silhouetted as one massive shadow. The lion reared back, and Luke advanced, flapping his jacket and yelling, making himself as large as possible.

The lion roared in return, and Luke contemplated flight in his own animal depths; but the human surface detected a fearful note in the cat's rage, and Luke swung his guitar into position. When his coat dropped, the cat whirled to regroup. Trying not to think, Luke struck the most dissonant, explosive notes he could, splaying his fingers haphazardly, perfect even at playing awful.

The mountain lion—though he knew it couldn't have—fixed him with a cold stare. Then, whimpering, it sped off until it was no longer visible from the top of the cliff.

Luke's jacket had fallen to the ground. He picked it up and wrapped it around himself. The sun had finally set and the Blue Ridge was bitterly cold.

About a hundred yards down the trail opened up again, leading down to a part of the valley farther to the east. The feeling of invincibility that came from winning the age-old conflict of man versus nature had stuck with him until he'd looked his predicament in the mirror. True, he was below the mist, but the fact that he could see no light from either direction only made things worse. Where exactly was he?

Luke gripped his guitar like a life preserver. He had no earthly idea.

But he had no trouble with unearthly ideas. Without willing it, he was thinking about his father; tears began to well up in his eyes as he imagined how casually he'd contemplated Christopher's death. Weeping not for himself or his father, or for what they never had, but for what Luke never knew they had. He'd been consumed with himself that first night he'd broached the idea, in the Second Year of Mary when Luke was nineteen years old.

"I'm not going to college, Dad," was how he opened.

Christopher parried. "Why not?"

"I want to be a troubador."

"A what?"

"A wandering musician. I want to travel the roads and play for people."

After that, Christopher had sat Luke down as calmly as possible before exploding. He had point after point and couldn't get them out fast enough: there was no longer such a thing as a troubador, he would have no way to make money, no future, he'd be abandoning his life for a hopeless quixotic fantasy. The rant must have taken root somewhere, but the conscious Luke was too excited to sit still.

When Christopher had finished yelling he sank into a more practical tone. The Appalachians, he said, were deadly. There was exposure to worry about, not to mention viruses, wild animals, and the distinct possibility of starvation that he assured would come from Luke's total lack of preparedness. Luke waved off every accusation. He could protect himself, he said; nothing bad ever happened to troubadors.

His mother had laughed at first, then stood stunned when Luke continued to insist he was serious. After that she had sat and cried while her husband held her and looked at his son as though he were a murderer.

Then he'd had to tell Mary. That had been the hard part.

They were engaged, or had been.

Luke paused to take several deep breaths. A few solitary rays of daylight were snuffed out as he watched, and the moon had begun to rise behind him. Not full, a waning gibbous with no particular symbolism. The chilly air pressed around his body and his teeth began to chatter. He'd never been so hungry in his life; not even the cold was so terrible as the knowledge that there was no way out of it. He was trapped—he might well be cold forever. For the rest of his life, however long that would be.

Walking again, seeing the valley walls inch past him, he realized that he wasn't trapped entirely—the guitar was still with him. That was when something preposterous occurred to him.

The thought of burning his instrument for fuel didn't provoke sadness or anger because it couldn't possibly happen: a wandering musician with no music was a man without a soul. He'd followed the guitar to the mountains; it was a piece of himself. To burn it would be nauseating, like severing a digit.

But it was cold, very cold. The chill was numbing. Luke could vividly feel the sensation of collapsing on the valley floor to sleep for days, then waking up to find himself too weak to walk before slipping again into permanent unconsciousness.

About then the mountain lion skidded down the slope and sped toward him from behind. It was feet away before it growled to betray its presence; by the time Luke spun around, they collided. The lion, a ball of spit and slashing claws, bowled the weakened Luke over into the grass; his guitar flew from his hand and skittered along the path. A claw slashed his cheek and blood began to flow.

He had already been cut in more places by the time he unified his existence with the utter shock of the attack. His first impulse was to wrestle with the beast, and he wrapped his arms around the lion's body, trying to force it into submission. The creature thrashed and threw him off, though they separated in the process, giving Luke his opening to stagger to his feet and try to flee.

He made it three feet. The lion pounced at his leg and Luke moaned with the agony and unfairness of it all as he felt teeth sink into flesh. Inadvertently shifting his weight to his wounded leg, he crumpled to the ground. In a flash the cat was once again tearing him apart.

"Do you know what happened at the end?" Mary said, without looking at him.

"Orpheus loses Eurydice. He looks back at her when he wasn't supposed to."

"That's not the end of the story." She still wouldn't meet his gaze. "Orpheus swears off love forever. But he gets a few nymphs following him. They learn he's not going to love him and they tear . . . him . . . apart." She slapped him between every word, tears welling up behind her cold façade. After she'd finished, she stumbled away, masking her sobs.

Luke realized, in the midst of shock as overwhelming as the pain, that he was about to let somebody else determine the ending of his story.

He brought his right knee up and struck the lion in the gut; to his surprise, it doubled backward, and Luke, rejoicing in the mercy, kicked viciously with his good right leg. The creature skidded and dropped. Luke wasted no time—in seconds his assailant would leap at him again. Bleeding from too many places, more places than he cared to count, he tried to step onto his left leg. Pain shot through it and he realized the lion's teeth must have hit bone and nerve. Dragging it behind him, he began to stagger, heading toward escape—by chance, toward the guitar.

The mountain lion roared behind him, it was on its feet. Luke had struck no more than a glancing blow.

The last bard on Earth dropped to his knees and reached for his Thracian lyre. He'd made a series of stupid choices but he would follow them until the end.

He never found the first chord.

When the predator was feet from him, he screamed, choked on the sound, and swung the guitar like a club.

Two sickening sounds told him he had struck home: the crack of wood on bone and the terrible splintering of the wood on itself as the siding and framework of the instrument crumpled into tinder. The lion whimpered and collapsed sideways, its eyes fluttering shut.

Luke hauled himself to his feet between wracking sobs. In the back of his mind he knew the creature was stunned at best, but he could think of nothing but what he had lost.

Taking the classical route, he began to run. Every step

sent a bolt of pain ricocheting through his leg; he felt like his bones were grinding together, like his senses had turned against him. He dimly recalled reading that the human body had a threshold for pain, and once it was reached, the system would overload and die from shock. This was a situation his father had neglected, though it must have occurred to him after Luke's departure, along with practically everything else.

A step. A knife of suffering that managed to be both sharp and dull. I've been a damn fool, he thought. I never read the ends of the myths. Orpheus always loses.

Ahead of him, he could see a jagged ravine, about as wide as he was tall.

Behind him, the mountain lion's legs were beginning to move.

He was clutching his guitar, the shattered remains of all he'd ever had. The jagged edge bounced beside him as he ran.

He blocked his leg out. The pain didn't exist; he willed himself to know how much worse the loss of the guitar would make him suffer. He couldn't even consider his circumstances; he had to make the jump. There was nothing else.

The lion growled behind Luke as he skidded to the edge of the precipice and hurled himself forward, limbs spinning, into the abyss. He avoided further damage to the guitar by flinging his right arm out to grasp the opposite ledge; his left arm bounced off the rock and he scrambled to find purchase. Every bump of his left leg against the cliff face was excruciating as he fought for a hold. He didn't know how far he had to fall because he would never look long enough to find out. At long last he managed to lodge the toe of his right shoe into a crevice, and begin hauling his way up.

The battered lion was right behind him on the opposite ledge, but Luke's mind was full. With both legs knocking on the wall, he dragged his upper body by inches, kicking with whatever leg was necessary, whether or not it tortured him.

After minutes he lay panting on a ridge of grass; after several more he was able to turn himself around.

The beast was not moving, nor growling, nor indicating anything; it stood, staring at its quarry in perhaps the most terrifying action of all. Luke knew he had managed to pummel it, or it would have been able to make the jump. He raised what had once been a guitar and was now an ornate weapon, stained with flecks of blood from two sources.

The lion didn't rise to the bait. Instead, it slunk off along the path Luke would have followed had he continued unabated. Luke was not relieved; it knew the way around.

Guided by his left leg, Luke tumbled over and prostrated himself in defeat. Everything he hadn't wanted to believe had come back to haunt him. He recalled how he had felt a week ago, yesterday, a few minutes prior. He wanted to laugh raucously and mock himself; he wanted to throw up. It was so easy to see now: since leaving Appomattox, the only people who had listened to him play were those who had thought he was begging. Some had teased and insulted him; one man in South Carolina had beaten him up for disturbing the peace on his street. There were no troubadors left because there was no longer anyone willing to be persuaded to feel; emotion was long gone from the entity of humanity.

And what he had left behind; Mary had shown him that. The sheer hatred in her last words was Luke's worst memory, the reason he remained unable to finish her song. He had left his father knowing nothing of his son's endangered life; he might have hastened his death. He had balked at the dangers of the mountains and hadn't even considered how he would eat. Now, here he was, under assault, starving, bleeding—

—and so cold he would consider burning his guitar.

Looking at the broken pile of wood, Luke feverishly connected strands in his mind. It was far from over.

Animals hated fire. That was pure common sense. There was something about the chaos they couldn't wrap their minds around. More practically, the heat taught them quickly to back away. Luke, praying his opponent was a quick learner, tore two lengthy splints from the instrument's shattered body. Still sprawled across the ground, he began scratching them together at right angles. He would prove them wrong; he would slap Mary and Christopher back in their faces. They said he was unprepared, but he was the master now.

Sparks jumped from the connecting points and Luke sawed harder, begging the wood to catch ablaze. It wasn't happening fast enough—how long could the route around the gash be?

The mountain lion appeared out of nowhere, leaping so mightily it completely overshot Luke, who sprang to his feet, blocking the numbing needles in his leg. It became so painful he could not even consider it, so, in a way, it dropped out of sight. Shifting backward into a defensive position, Luke held the jagged embers before his body.

"Come on," he murmured, "Come on, goddamit . . . "

The lion switched its weight and pounced, but Luke was ready for it; stabbing upward with one of the wooden shards at the moment the beast was inches from his face, he cut a jagged gash into its stomach and felt blood pouring over his hands. The wood, soaked in lifeblood, slipped from his hands; when the lion retaliated by hurling its bulk into Luke, he thrust the wood between his eyes and his enemy's. A claw reached out and scratched the sparking splinter; in a flash it was alight. The lion reared backward off Luke and dropped back—unsteady, losing blood, but determined to fight on.

Luke was unready for the heat of the flame and dropped it; fortune ordained the guitar's remains as the landing spot. The dry body caught on fire instantly; Luke seized the neck of the torch and felt the former string warming—in too short a time they would be too hot to touch.

He swung the flaming guitar in a wide arc and caught the lion across the neck, burning away his old life.

The lion roared and jumped away, regrouping and rounding on Luke again. He was ready for it and slashed the fire at its legs, kicking his new life away from under him. He was here, now, Luke McKinney, nothing more than a man. Evenly matched. A real monk now.

The mountain lion was reduced to a whirlwind of slashing claws and teeth; Luke continued to bat it away with his torch, though his grip was becoming unbearable.

The beast's teeth were bared. Luke forgot everything and gambled for once with a life that was well and truly his own—

—he sent the fireball spinning through the frigid air—

—the lion was hit, roaring, whimpering, its fur set burning—

—it staggered, lost its balance at the edge of the ravine, and plummeted out of sight. The guitar followed it down.

Luke listened for a while, but no sound returned. He thought how nice it would be to see Mary again. Then, bleeding, limping, dragging his injured leg, he headed up the path, his teeth chattering, wrapping his bloody jacket around himself. He was an ascetic. He could stand one more night in the woods.

so much they never knew

camille currey

NOAH WAS ON THE STEPS OF ST. CHRISTOPHER'S Lutheran Intermediate. Every day he took one full moment to think of how odd it was that a Lutheran school should be named St. anything, considering that worship of the saints was one of the reasons Martin Luther broke away from the Catholic Church. Then he took another full moment to think that intermediate was such an odd word, and why couldn't they just use "middle school" like every other place in the world.

Deciding that this was out of his control, he walked through the large oak doors—obviously meant to look older than they feasibly could have been—to his spring semester of sixth grade. So far, middle school wasn't that bad. At the very least, none of the eighth graders had beaten him up. But he didn't really have many people that he considered close friends; he'd left *them* in Minnesota back in July.

Noah walked into his first period literature class. Everything seemed to be in order, but Noah had that feeling. It was that feeling that you get right before something big happens, like saying your line as the squash in the Thanksgiving play, or right before you go down the big hill on a roller coaster; it was that feeling of cautious excitement. As Noah's eyes landed on a mop of dirty blond hair, he realized why. There was a new boy. So Noah decided to be that kid, the kid that makes the first move.

"Hi, I'm Noah. This is Michelle's seat, there is an open one by me, though," he said cautiously.

"I'm Jack," said the boy simply.

Noah moved to where they would be sitting and Jack, after a moment of sizing Noah up, followed.

"So where are you from?" Noah asked politely.

"Nevada," Jack replied throwing back some of the hair that had fallen into his face.

"Cool! Like, Las Vegas?"

"No."

"Oh."

Both boys fell into silence and kept to themselves as their ancient, nasal-voiced teacher, Mrs. Zilkey, called the class to order and began the morning's lesson. They were reading something about Saturdays, and it seemed like nobody was paying any attention. Finally, after forty-five excruciating minutes, the bell rang.

"People just calm yourselves for a second. Stop packing up; I have papers to pass out to all of you. Now this is about swine flu. This is very serious, people. People, people, please. I need your attention here, swine flu is a very serious disease," Mrs. Zilkey said hurriedly, spittle in the corners of her mouth.

Jack mumbled something Noah didn't catch. He turned from the decrepit woman to his new friend and asked, "What did you say?"

"It's all a conspiracy between the news channels, the doctors, and the Anti-Catholicism League," Jack stated as if it were something that everyone knew.

"What?" Noah asked, stunned.

"You know, the news channels' ratings were plummeting, so they got together with the doctors and the Anti-Catholicism League and set up swine flu to improve the ratings," Jack said conspiratorially.

"But wait, aren't the doctors the ones trying to stop swine flu? And what is the Anti-Catholicism League?" Noah asked, eyebrows pulled tightly together.

"No, man," Jack shook his head slowly. "The doctors are used to making a ton of money, right?"

Noah nodded.

"Well," Jack continued, "with the recession and everything they needed a way to save their BMWs and beach houses, so they made the disease then partnered up with the news channels so that they could use their press badges to get it into otherwise restricted areas. Plus the government totally picked up on this. *That's* why it's taking so long to make the vaccines." At Noah's blank look, Jack rolled his eyes and plundered on, "They're using the vaccines for mind control. They thought that this was a great opportunity to legally insert the devices. They're arguing that this is all perfectly okay because people are taking the vaccines of their 'own volition.'"

"But what about the Anti-Catholicism League?"

"There's this group of people that hate Catholics. They've been trying to eradicate them for years, but it's hard because a lot of Catholics don't believe in using birth control, so they multiply at a super rate! The ACL or 'The League' pretty much have most of them rounded up in Mexico now, and the swine flu was one of their attempts to get in, massacre, and get out. They get really bad indigestion from the salsa, see, so they couldn't stay long enough to eat a meal," Jack said pointedly.

By this point in time, Noah wasn't sure if Jack was being serious. He was going to point out that people did actually eat other things in Mexico beside chips and salsa, but it didn't matter because now they had to run to P.E.

"C'mon Jack! If we're late, Coach Chambers will make us run suicides till we puke!" He took off running down the stairs toward the elementary and the gym. "You think I'm kidding," Noah huffed, "but he made that foreign exchange student blow chunks everywhere last Tuesday."

At this, Jack paled slightly and began to run faster.

After a grueling workout, the boys changed and headed off to world history. As they walked in, Jack was jarred by the sight of a colossally pregnant woman at the front of the classroom. She had short brown hair straightened and flipped at the end with a multitude of highlights streaking through it.

"Stop staring. She hates it when people do that," Noah admonished. "Come on, we don't have assigned seats in here."

Jack followed with glances back at the massive woman trying to confirm that someone could actually become that big. It was not like Jack had never seen a pregnant woman before; he did have two younger siblings. It just didn't look right on this woman. She was barely five feet tall with very thin arms and legs. He imagined that the size of her midsection accounted for at least double the size of the rest of her.

"I know, it's *weird,* right?" Noah asked, privy to the thoughts of his new friend.

"It's just . . . just . . . " he trailed off.

"Yeah I know, and believe it or not this is baby number five. I heard that she and her husband are trying for a boy. And I heard from Marty's older brother—he's in *high school* now—that she just keeps getting bigger and bigger and bigger and he said that if she gets pregnant again then they are going to have to give her her own zip code!"

"Shut up! She's coming over here," said Jack, jerking his head toward the waddling woman.

"Hello, you must be Jack Lancaster. I'm Mrs. Hartjen and I teach all of the intermediate history courses here at St. Christopher's. I am so looking forward to instructing you for the next two and a half years," she cocked her head, a picket fence of teeth gleaming.

Jack was mesmerized by the focus of her blue eyes as she cocked her head to the side like a bird watching a particularly defenseless, albeit juicy, worm. She was obviously part of some infamous *Them*. The question was: Which one?

Jack's question was quickly answered as Mrs. Hartjen waddled back to the front of the class and wrote: THE MIDDLE AGES: FEUDALISM, CODE OF CHIVALRY, RELIGION, AND THE CRUSADES in what Noah could only describe as girl writing—messy in a pretty kind of way, but legible to the extreme. Noah heard his father say once that women want you to know what they are saying but they also want you to have a little trouble figuring it out, and if it didn't reflect in their handwriting then his name was Jahosaphat. (His father's name was Keith.)

"Class, can anyone tell me what you think of when I say, the 'Middle Ages'?" Mrs. Harjen asked, smiling demurely.

Kaalah's hand shot into the air and she didn't wait to be called on before blurting out, "Knights in shining armor!"

"I'll be your knight in shining armor, Kay," stage-whispered a handsome and intimidating boy in the back row.

"Shut up, Colton," snapped the attractive blonde.

"*Enough!*" shrieked Mrs. Hartjen, reclaiming the class's attention. "Now," she continued, "the most important thing to remember whilst studying the Middle Ages, Medieval Times, or 'Dark Ages' as they are often called is— "

"That they never existed," supplied another male voice from the back of the class.

"Mr. Lancaster, I am sure that I need not remind you that you *Never* get a second chance at first impressions," crooned the very frustrated and slightly crazed teacher.

"Well, I think that in school people should learn the facts, and the fact is that the Middle Ages never happened," Jack shrugged.

"Well, Mr. Lancaster, then how on earth do you explain all of the history that came out of this time period? If the Middle Ages did not exist, then what year are we really living in? Hmm?" she tutted, the hormones rearing their ugly head as each question climbed octaves in leaps and bounds, with her head shaking and streaked hair frazzled.

"Well, ma'am, we are indeed living in the year 1712 AD."

At his proclamation, the class roared with laughter. Colton actually hit the ground and began to gasp, clutching his sides. There were only three people in that room who managed to exercise some control over themselves: Mrs. Hartjen glared at Jack; Jack stood, solemn faced, staring right back; and Noah sat, mouth agape, completely shocked by the way in which his new friend had spoken to a teacher.

"Jack. Sweetheart. I think that you must be confused. Here at St. Christopher's we don't really joke around in class. I will however let you off, this being your first day." She had reverted to being sickeningly sweet.

"Thank you, Mrs. Hartjen. I really appreciate that, but I hate to see a civil injustice. This is like trying to deny Troy."

Why? Why God? I finally get one friend. One stinking friend, and he is completely off his rocker. Why! thought Noah.

Well, Noah, you asked me for a friend, you never specified that you wanted one of the sane persuasion, Noah could hear God's booming voice answer him.

"I'll be sure to clarify next time," Noah audibly grumbled.

During Noah's divine exchange, Mrs. Hartjen had phoned the principal and was now gesturing wildly into the receiver.

"I DON'T CARE HOW MUCH HIS PARENTS DONATED TO PREVENT HIS EXPULSION! GET HIM THE heck OUT OF MY CLASS, GLEN! STRESS IS NOT GOOD FOR MY BABY, AND SO HELP ME IF SOMETHING GOES WRONG I WILL TAKE YOUR B-U-T-T TO THE CLEANERS!" Slamming the receiver back down on the hook, looking more worn than any of the students had ever seen her, Mrs. Hartjen rounded on the boy who was the source of her anxiety.

"She does know that we know how to spell 'butt' right?" questioned Colton, who had somehow managed to worm his way into the seat next to Kaalah, who promptly rolled her eyes.

Derrek, who lived for a classroom in uproar, shouted across the twelve different conversations in the room, "Hey! Jack, why don't you explain your theory!"

"Well," Jack began, "I am sure that you have all heard

of the Anti-Catholicism League." Upon receiving blank stares, Jack heaved a sigh of exasperation. "The Anti-Catholicism League are, in part, responsible for the invention and spread of swine flu, but that is another facet to be explored later. Anyway, the Anti-Catholicism League started in protest to the Medieval Movement put into effect by Pope Otto III.

"He basically wanted to be remembered as the first pope of the new millennium; his only problem was that he lived during the early 700s. We all know that Rome invented our current calendar, so under the instruction of Pope Otto, the historians fudged the dates some 300 years. He also employed several writers to work closely with the historians to create fictional historical characters that over time were thought to have actually lived. By the reaction of our lovely teacher you can see that this propaganda has infected the minds of millions.

"But don't worry, not only do you now know the truth, but you don't have to worry about dying in 2012. That's not for another 300 years! Actually, that is just another conspiracy set up by the FBI. They have all of your phones tapped so that they can tell whether the mass state of panic is at all escalating. And . . . " but Jack never got to forewarn his new classmates about the horrors of the FBI, because at that moment the blustering, red-faced principal, Glen Kieshnick, stormed into the room.

At some point during Jack's dissertation on the Middle Ages, Mrs. Hartjen had sunk to the floor of the classroom, silent sobs wracking through her. Mr. Kieshnick took in the zoo before him, and settled on his frazzled employee.

He sighed and called, "Jack Lancaster."

Jack jumped down from the desk and shot a winning grin over his shoulder, a very knowing glint in his eye.

Jack never returned to school. Rumors flew like lightning from one end of the hall to the other and back again. Some claimed that the Anti-Catholicism League had finally gotten him; some claimed that it was not the Anti-Catholics, but the Catholics who wanted him dead for slandering one of their Popes, while others (probably started by the teachers) said that he was only kicked out of school.

It didn't matter. None of the children could answer the phone for weeks without yelling obnoxiously, "FBI, I know you're there!"

70 year curse

olga garduño

HE TAKES A LONG DRAG FROM HIS PIPE. He finds the damn spring in his chair is bothering his back. He gets up in a bad mood and decides to go bother his afternoon nurse, whom he thought served for two things: for little, and for nothing. He sees his electric wheelchair from the corner of his eye, but ignores it knowing it will only upset me more if he doesn't use it.

He is a grumpy old man. I think it is due to his idea that he is going to die tomorrow. According to him no one in his family from his great-great-great-great grandaddy ever survived past the age of 70 and he is one day away from that horrible age. He is a firm believer that it is a curse set upon his family by his great-great-great-great grandaddy's lover who only came to find out *she* was the lover when she was 40 years into the affair. This only proved his point that women are good for nothing, and his wife's sudden disappearance only came to prove his point.

George straggles over to the front desk where the nurses clock in.

"Where's Anabel?" George growls.

"I don't know, George, I don't think she's here yet," Amy the young receptionist replies softly; she has had her couple run ins with George and she knows that it is best to keep away from him.

"I can't hear a damn word you said," George reproaches. "Ah! Forget you, you ain't know nothing," he blows her off and continues his straggle. "I have to do everything myself around here, these good for nothing . . . " he murmurs to himself as he gets to the linen closet where he gets a couple of fresh sheets and a blanket to cover his window.

He passes by the entrance of the TV room before getting to his bedroom and looks around, practically everyone in the old folks home is there, but him. They are all strangers to him. He didn't think it was worth while making friends since he is about to die; he almost pitied them and their weak attempt at happiness while playing bingo and chess.

"See you stupids," George murmurs under his breath before continuing his death walk.

He dumps the sheets on the bed.

"George?" I ask, as I knock on the door.

"What took you so goddamn long?" he reproaches.

I walk into the room to find George at his bed, packing his belongings.

"What are you doing, George?" I look around seeing that the window in his room is covered with a blanket from the linen room. I walk over to the window to take it off.

"Stop!!" George yells, walking over to stop me. "What the hell are you doing?"

"What do you mean what am I doing?" I reproach. "This isn't supposed to be here."

"I want it there and you're gonna leave it there."

"No sir I'm not."

"I'm about to die and you can't even leave a damn blanket on the window?"

"For Pete's sake!" I exclaim. "George, you are not going to die. I REPEAT, NOT GOING TO DIE!"

"Yes, I am," he reverts. "Now stop your yammering and help me pack my things. I don't want anyone to get my stuff so after I die I need you to go and burn this bag in the woods somewhere. Oh, and make sure you see that it all burns!"

"George," I stop, realizing that he truly believes he will die tomorrow. "Okay."

"What?"

"I will do it, George."

"Good, now I won't have to do it myself."

"What do you mean? You were going to do it yourself?!"

"Don't worry about it. Why do you think they called me Sparky in the Army?" George gives me one of his wild looks. "Stop standing there or leave."

"Fine I'll leave," I say while leaving the dark bare room.

I come back an hour later to find George in bed with his Vietnam vet uniform. All the lights are off, except for the light on the night stand next to his bed.

"George?" I say as I move closer to the bed, there is no reply. "George quit it." I stare at his almost childlike face, he seems at rest.

"What?!" George exclaims.

I jump up five feet in the air.

"Jeez, George!" I exclaim.

"What do you want? Can't you see I'm on my death bed?!"

"Do you want dinner or not? Everyone is eating right now. Come down to the cafeteria."

"Are you blind or what?!" George says, half sitting up in bed. "I am a dead man; there is no point in me eating if I will die tomorrow!"

"George, come eat. You won't die, I promise."

"I said I ain't goin'!"

I leave and decide to forget about him for a while, all he needs is getting past tomorrow.

• • • • •

This dumb nurse! Why are they all so goddamn stupid? I curl over to the side and try to sleep through my death. I'm not sure of my death's schedule, but I expect it to be around midnight; it's eleven. I stare at the light under the door and every so often I see the shadow of people's feet going by the door. I find it almost dizzying, all my life I have spent trying to forget this awful day, but who gives a damn. I fall asleep and come to wake up with the awful scene of the last time I saw my wife. I knew she was going to leave, I was so drunk. I knew what she was doing though. I screamed for her; she didn't come this time and I got up angry ready to scream at her—the thing I knew how to do best. When I got to her bedroom everything was vanished; there was nothing there, her perfumes her clothes were all gone. I ran all around the house. She had taken my son too! She had taken everything except my filthy things. I walked into the kitchen to find that the only thing there was a plate of my favorite dish, sitting there on the table all alone. I began to cry and I threw everything in my sight. I kept the dish though and I held it and cried. I knew I had finally done it. I knew they were gone forever.

I lie there in the dark lonely room and I grab the pillow as hard as I can. Every time I remember that scene my heart aches. What hurts more is that I haven't seen her since. I tried tracking her down, but it was pointless. She was the kind of woman whose decisions were final and she always thought about the consequences before going through with them.

I realize that I'm still in the cold dark room. I sit up in bed and look at the clock; it is three in the morning. I lie back down and I look up at the ceiling. I remember when I was a little boy, I would lay in bed in the dark, terrified, and I would cry and cry, but there was no response—only the sad cricket outside my window singing his disconsolate tune. When I turned sixteen I ran away from home and joined the military. I lied about my age, telling them I was 18. My face said otherwise, but the Vietnam War was in the works and they needed man power. I was placed in infantry; I hated it so I worked hard to become a first lieutenant, and by the age of 18 I was no longer a walking target. I worked hard in the army. I became the best, but our defeat was the worst thing that happened to me. My aspirations of being a victorious general were crushed. I left, which is when I met my wife, Martha. She was beautiful, but I was ruined.

I open my eyes and realize I had fallen asleep. I turn and look at the clock and see it is eight in the morning.

A soft knock comes from the door.

"Great . . . time for meds" I murmur.

"Morning, George," Lupe waddles in. "I brought your medication."

"Yeah Yeah . . . " I say. "I won't be needing it though, so don't bother me and take that muffin top out of my room!"

"I ain't leaving 'til you take it," Lupe becomes agitated.

"You no comprendo? You stupid-o?!" I glare. "Me-o No taking-o the medication-o!!"

"This is the last straw George! Take the medication or I'm going to sedate you."

"I want to see you try!"

Before I can say Sacajawea, she has me pinned down and is shooting me up. I feel extreme drowsiness; I can't help but fall asleep.

• • • • •

I decide to go check up on George since I heard he had been sedated earlier. He is still asleep. I have always wondered why George never talks about his family; he always cringes whenever I say the word. Once a young man came to visit. He asked if George was still alive, but he never made the slightest move toward meeting him.

I decide to go check his files for background information; hopeful that maybe I can find some relatives that can support him. There isn't much though; there are only relatives who have passed away and it seems to be that he was sent to the home by the police. He had run over the neighbors' cat and apparently assaulted a clerk at Albertson's. He was too much of a threat to public safety. There is no information about immediate relatives though; it says he had one son, but no name or address. I decide to take it upon myself to search for his missing family.

• • • • •

I open my eyes and it takes me a couple of minutes to focus, I feel extremely groggy and I feel all my body aching, definite sign that I am still alive. I wrestle over the covers turning my body and looking at the clock; it's six. I have approximately six hours left, great. I sit there and realize that I still have basic human necessities. As I walk back from the pot I decide to take a quick peek outside at the sunset, it looks like a good sunset to die to.

When I left the military I got a job as a tow truck

driver and on the weekends I would take my boy to the lake; he loved riding in the truck. We would go out there fishing until the sun went down, and we would sit on the edge of the river and watch the sunset before it set.

After Martha took him I didn't hear from him until one Christmas Eve when he came by and visited me with his wife when he was around 35. We tried to stay in contact, but we argued too much. I decided to disappear from his life for good; it served us best.

I walk toward my secret nook beside the TV in my room, I take out a Cuban cigar I have been saving for a special occasion and sit down on the chair in the corner of the room next to window. I light the cigar; it is too dry—stupid crappy cigar, damn Cubans. While sitting there smoking that crappy cigar I remember my grandfather. When I was about five he would come pick me up on Sundays and take me to church. Of course, after we would go to the nearest pub and he would have me sit on the bar next to him and a couple of his friends and wait for him while he drank and smoked. He would get so drunk sometimes that I would have to take him by the hand and lead him home. My mother despised him, but I knew he could never hurt a fly. He died of a heart attack when I was nine. By then I was a pub regular: I swept the bar and took out the trash. After my grandfather died we moved towns. Apparently, my grandfather owed too much money and my dad didn't want to get the short end of the stick.

I feel sick of thinking. I grab the remote and turn the TV on to the history channel. A documentary about aliens is on, stupid aliens. Back in my day no one gave a damn about aliens—stupid generation—they got too much time on their hands. I flip through the channels. I watched a little of *Chelsea Lately* and I'm pretty sure if I keep watching it any longer my eyes will begin to bleed. I keep flipping only to see that stupid yellow sponge I left on it. Maybe this is what will cause my death. It could even make headlines: Old man killed by an evil yellow sponge. Five minutes went by but no cigar, so I turn off that brain-vegetating crap.

I walk over to the bed and lie down. I check the time, nine o'clock.

• • • • •

"Hey George," I say. "I brought you some food. I bet you're starving."

"I told you I didn't want anything! Leave it on the table over there," he grumbles.

"Okay, let me know if you need anything," I smile. "Good night."

I can't wait until tomorrow, he is about to get the surprise of his life.

• • • • •

I pounce at the food like a starving animal. I've always eaten fast because that's what I was trained to do in the military, but this time I'm not even chewing. The food finally does its magic. I feel sleepy again; I lie down again. I look up at the ceiling.

"I guess this is it," I murmur to myself.

My life's events flash before my eyes—everything from the good times to my lows.

I close my eyes at 10:12. Never to wake again; only to a pit of eternal nothingness.

• • • • •

"Excuse me, where can I find Anabel?"

"Oh, hi, I'm so glad you made it," I say. "He's been very depressed lately; follow me he's over here." I lead the stranger through the halls, finally reaching the room. I open the door and take down the blanket from the window. The stranger walks right up to the side of his bed, looking painfully at him. Then reaches toward him, but doesn't follow through with the action.

• • • • •

I feel the presence of someone and the light bothers my eyes, so maybe I don't make it to heaven. I don't want to rush the deep happiness I feel inside so I keep my eyes closed. I get my thoughts in order of what I want to tell God, but curiosity beats my thoughts. I open my eyes. I feel myself get lightheaded, I break out in a cold sweat, my jaw snaps shut, my arms tingle as if I had fire-ants biting them, and then an extreme pain flows through my chest. Only one word could describe my joy, "Martha," I gasp.

• • • • •

I guess the curse did come true, I did die but the hope of a chance of happiness and forgiveness made me fight the mental curse I had set upon myself. It took Martha and me about six months to decide to get back together. Apparently, I wasn't the only one who suffered.

It has been nine years since the last time I went to Raisin Ranch Old Folks Home. Anabel comes and visits us often and if it weren't for her I would really be premature maggot food.

"Happy 79th birthday, George!!" everyone shouted.

"Are there any curse's we should know about, before we start singing?" Anabel laughed.

"Well actually . . . " I considered.

DUM

sean kelner

I ALWAYS WONDERED WHAT HAPPENS to us after we die. During my final night as John Red, I pondered about the after-life for hours, my mind satiated with horrible thoughts and feelings. These thoughts and feelings didn't leave until after I had done it; I killed myself that night. These thoughts and feelings were replaced by curiosity and anticipation. As my vision blackened, my world spun and I realized I was about to find out first-hand what happens to us after we die.

It was my religion and curiosity that motivated me

throughout my life, and, ironically, killed me. I was a scientist, more specifically a micro-biologist. I studied tiny organisms, seeking evidence of evolution. I wondered about God, I wondered about heaven, and I wondered about hell. I wanted answers and my career seemed like a source for those answers.

My life was prodigious. I lived in an extravagant house in Massachusetts. I had the keys to a Porsche and a closet the size of a master bedroom. However, despite my extensive repository of material items, I was not satisfied. Perhaps my biggest flaw as John Red was my discontent.

My family was unorthodox. My father had the emotion of petrified wood and my mother seemed as though she could not stand to be happy. I remember my last conversation with my father; it was about trash:

"John?" my dad said.

"Yeah?" I replied, aggravated. I could always tell when my dad was going to ask me to do something. It made me mad that he wouldn't just ask. He insisted on dancing around the question.

"You know . . . it's trash night." Our neighborhood's trash was picked up once a week, and in order for your trash to get picked up you had to drag your trash cans to the curb.

"Yeah, I know. I'm going to take it out."

"Oh, well I was just wondering if you knew it was trash night, but okay." My dad acted surprised even though I had been taking out the trash for years.

My brother Casey had a wife and son. I remember one of the last times I talked to my brother. We were at the gym:

"So, Casey, how's your job going?" I asked.

"Eh, it's going." He replied, seemingly eager to change the subject.

"I hope you're doing well." My brother often had a depressed vibe about him so I found myself trying to comfort him a lot.

"Yeah, man, I'm doing fine." He replied, laughing. My brother laughed, but I knew he would soon start to vent.

"Okay, I'm glad."

"But you know . . . mom is still trying to get me to come to the house all the time." I knew something would be wrong in his life.

"Yeah, she doesn't get it does she? You and Lauren both want to cut the cord already and move on."

"Exactly," he replied quietly. To my surprise, that's all that we said to each other that day.

• • • • •

My sister Lauren was an ambitious college student and a waitress. She had a smile that could light up the whole room and a laugh that was like hearing your favorite song. Unfortunately, I cannot remember the last time I talked to her, and it eats me up inside.

To me my siblings were saviors. There was not a problem or issue too great for us to get through together. I still believe that they were my best friends. I missed my family dearly, for they had all died prematurely: My parents died of heart attacks, my sister died in a car accident, and my brother committed suicide. These losses were a series of horrible, traumatic events.

Since the loss of my family, I was always lonely. The days went by slower and slower. Eventually I couldn't think of anything except my brother and sister. These thoughts and feelings were overwhelming, so much that I lost my job after several jaded months of unanimated self-destruction. Everything I owned seemed to remind me of my family and their absence. But drinking helped me forget.

One thing I can certainly remember was my last day

of work. From the time that I woke up to the time I went to sleep, I felt great. I went out to eat for breakfast which was unusual for me. I even remember the waitress and my order.

"Hi, I'd like the French toast with two sunny-side-up eggs and three pieces of beacon." I asserted with a smug grin across my face.

"Okay. I assume you're a morning person, judging from that mischievous smile." She replied, snootily.

"Nope, I'm just quitting my job."

"Well, alright, mister." She said, while giving me a strange look. I thought it was funny that I was happy about quitting my job. It made me wonder if this job was really a positive thing or not. I mean I'd been at it for five years; maybe I just wasted my time. All these thoughts were just a taste of the brainstorm-like mental conversations I was having.

Soon after I ate and left the restaurant, I arrived at work. I worked in a state-of-the-art venue that seemed as though it was just too clean. To me it looked more like a hotel than an office. Never the less I trudged up the stairs to the third floor, eager to talk to my boss. I marched down the white-tiled floors and eventually came to my boss's office. Her door tag read, "Dr. Maria Hutcheson." I opened the door and sat down in her nice leather waiting chair.

"Hi there, John, what can I do you for?" She said. Her bright smile and positive attitude ironically fueled my desire to quit.

"I'm quitting." I replied.

"Um, okay?" She looked as though she thought it was a joke, but after a few awkward seconds she realized I was dead serious and she began to explain what I should do before I left. She began reading out of her book full of procedures to tell me how to clean my office, but half-way through her speech, I interrupted her:

"Alright, as much as I'd love to stay and follow your stupid procedures, I've got a bar to crash in." Walking out of her office felt so great and it only got better.

In my frequent visits to the local bar, I met several poor, old friends like me. Some had lost everything, some just liked to have a good time. One of these friends was David. David was coincidentally a biologist; however, he was much more venerable in the world of science. He had written several volumes of books about botany and as a result became very rich. David had a wife and two daughters; he also had a marvelous house in a great neighborhood. He lost most of what he had in a domestic violence court battle with his wife. Another friend at the bar was Nick. Nick was an accountant for a major corporation in Massachusetts. He was a bachelor and was proud of it. He also had Porsche and he drove it like he was beating a deadline. Unlike me and David, Nick wasn't drinking away his problems, for he had none.

After several weeks of living off my savings and spending all day at bars, I found myself spiraling down to hit rock-bottom. For some reason I didn't mind. I suppose it was because I had lost it all. Unfortunately, my sketchy friendships through the bars couldn't replace my family, job, and health. I remember my last night as John Red superbly, although I wish I couldn't.

I remember stumbling through my front door, so far gone I couldn't have recited the alphabet. I remember the disgusting taste and numb feeling in my mouth and throat. I sat down in my leather recliner, near the fireplace. I opened up a box from my move into the house. From within the box I removed a black leather photo album. I morosely flipped through the pages of pictures, gawking at the images of my family. Tears glistened on my cheeks as I became thoughtless. I dropped the book in the fireplace, although there wasn't a fire. My vision was blurry and my knees weak. I rose from the chair and sauntered into my bathroom. I had spent weeks renovating my bathroom, but the modern lighting and precious tiles wouldn't impress me. I turned on the shower and collapsed into the bathtub, the water drenching me and my new, expensive clothes. I stripped down, already soaking wet. I wallowed in despondency for hours. Soon enough the only image in my mind was that of a bright light, God I presume. I envisioned my brother and sister and grabbed my razor. I closed my eyes and in a seemingly interminable feat, I ended my life. As the warmth evaporated from my body, the water still hitting me, I dreamed of heaven. Soon enough my world was black, yet I was still thinking.

I was practically conscious. I couldn't see, I couldn't speak, and I couldn't wake up. I was all thoughts. It was astonishing. I expected some sort of judging and Passover. However all that lay before me was this idiosyncratic darkness. The especially aberrant part of only being able to think is the inability to sleep. I was constantly aware of my circumstances. Although it was mystifying, my state led to some productive brainstorming. I thought about what I would say to God if he were to judge me. I thought about what I would say to my brother and sister if I saw them in heaven. I never once thought of the possibility of hell.

After what felt like eternity, a bright light reinstated the pitch-black darkness that once engorged my vision. Then I heard a deafening ringing in my ears. Finally, I felt as though I was being pulled molecule by molecule. The bright light dimmed and a tunnel-like object materialized before me. This tunnel shined a deep violet hue. At this moment I remembered a peculiar conversation I had with an acquaintance from college in a local Starbucks. We were both studying and at the sight of him laughing, I questioned him.

"What could possibly be funny about physics?" I said with sarcastic inquiry.

"This man John Wheeler theorized about a thing called a wormhole. (He chuckled.) He says they could lead to other dimensions or galaxies. He says they glow a radiant purple. It sounds more sci-fi to me than scientific." He explained.

"Ah, I see." Only a student in physics would laugh so hysterically at something like that, I thought to myself.

I was sucked into the wormhole, zooming down the incandescent hallway at unprecedented speeds. Oddly my thoughts were joyful because I could see again. However what I was seeing was not exactly pleasant. I felt as though I was on a rollercoaster. Eventually, the ride stopped and my vision blackened again, only this time I couldn't even think. I hoped for some spectacular divine encounter and was disheartened by the absence of such an event.

I aroused comfortably. I was lying in a Tempur–Pedic bed, with warm silk sheets draped over my body. I observed the room around me. It was strange, to say the least. The walls were made of a glistening alloy that seemed indestructible. Above me was a mine-field of lights that were dimmed, deep within the ceiling. There were windows, but they were tinted so dark that I could not see through them. The floor was surprisingly covered in the same tiles I had in my bathroom. The furniture within the room was extremely modern and most of it was made out of the same alloy as the walls. There was a desk, complete with a computer that seemed as though it belonged to the secretary of defense. There was also typical living room furniture allotted in a spacious fashion, as though it was from a magazine. I ventured through the loft to find that it was composed of only two rooms, the room in which I awoke and a living room. The room was outfitted with sleek, modern appliances and lighting. I was dazzled by all of these things. I thought I was dead, but apparently not.

I relaxed at my desk for a moment and was petrified by a greeting from the computer.

"Hello, John 4869," the computer said.

"Whoa . . . hello?" I replied confused.

"Today is Tuesday, February 16."

"Um, 2009?"

"ERROR," the computer replied. Apparently it didn't understand my question or it doesn't keep time.

"Would you like to know your e-mail status, John?"

"No, but I do have a few questions." I lied, I had countless questions.

"Am I dead?" I asked anxiously.

"No."

"Is this my loft?"

"Yes"

"Is this heaven?" I asked with a convoluted expression.

"No, this is hell, John 4869" The monotone voice of the computer echoed these words in my skull for several seconds. My stomach felt queasy and my palms were sweaty. I trudged to my bedroom and lay down for hours. My thoughts were embossed with the word "hell". I was seeking God, happiness, my family. I thought I could bring myself to them. I thought I could be in a better place, reunited with my siblings forever in the kingdom of God. The stress wrenched me from sleep.

I decided to leave the loft and excavate this "hell" that was apparently filled with modern design. I peered into my closet to find that my clothes were pristine. Designer suits and shoes of brands that I couldn't pronounce. I proudly waltzed out my loft to explore the world of hell. The halls of the apartment building were much like the halls of my loft. The walls were shiny metal and the lights were luminescent. I marched to the elevator and found that I was on the 100th floor; I had never lived so high up. I took the elevator down to the ground floor, which surprisingly took merely seconds. From the elevator I strolled through the lobby, which looked like the Sistine chapel. An old woman greeted me from the front desk. So far, hell seemed like a walk in the park. I walked outside the tented glass doors to find a marvelous, foreign world. The sky was a deep crimson, the sun was a bright blue, and the horizon was full of concrete jungle. The city was a modernized metropolis. The temperature must have been over one hundred degrees; it was the hottest I had ever felt. I walked down the sidewalk, sweating profusely. I discovered that there were cameras on all angles of every single intersection and corner I came to. Some of them appeared to be moving. I thought it strange that there were so many cameras, for everything was clean, and the city seemed crime free.

I concluded my exploration after walking close to one hundred blocks in a giant square. I was feeling famished and thirsty so I decided to stop at a restaurant. I strolled through the front door and sat down at the bar. An older woman approached me on the opposite side of the counter and took my order. As I waited for my meal, I peered around the other tables of the restaurant only to find several separate groups of elders conversing and waiting for their food as well. It was at that point that I noticed the peculiarity of the city. On my walk and now in the restaurant I hadn't seen anyone under the age of fifty. The city lacked diversity, but also crime and filth.

My food was delicious and my thirst was quenched. As I got up and walked toward the door, an older man invited me to sit at his table with several others. I accepted this invitation. I thought maybe I could learn a little more about this "hell" city.

"Hi, I'm John." I said politely.

"Hey, John, I'm Earl. I invited you to sit down because my friends and I here couldn't help but notice your youth. We'd like to ask you a few questions." He replied.

"Yeah, sure."

"So, how old are you?"

"Thirty." I hadn't felt young in years. Earl looked at his friends for a few moments.

"You could very well be the youngest person alive." I began to laugh but I became silent after I noticed their stern faces.

"You can't be serious. How could that possibly be?"

"Have you not watched the news in the past twenty years? You must live under a rock."

"No, I couldn't explain to you what I've been through in the past twenty-four hours. I'm not from here. I don't understand this predicament one bit, will you please explain?" They began to laugh amongst themselves.

"Alright John, I'll explain. It all started twenty years ago in 2010. The government decided to implement a new set of laws and began a program called DUM. These new laws allowed the government to put everyone out of work. The government controls where we are allowed to go and when. The letters in DUM stand for dehumanize, utilize, and maintain. The government has dehumanized us all by containing us within certain areas: our homes, neighborhoods, or cities. They have utilized us by using the money saved by not having to pay for schools and other government-funded industries on new modern infrastructure. The government is now maintaining this control by using police and military force."

"Alright that explains the city but what about the old age?"

"In the absence of human activity in public, a new, more powerful form of the influenza virus has formed. After the construction of modernized cities, like the one we live in, people were allowed to return to the streets. The unsuspecting population was plagued by this new disease. An estimated 99.7% of the country's population was at one point infected. The disease is especially dangerous because it permanently inhibits the reproductive system. The sterility of the infected is passed down genetically. This disease has destroyed the reproductive ability of the country and eventually it will destroy that of the world." I took close to a minute to try to comprehend this, and to reflect on what I just heard.

"Okay, so I could be one of the few humans remaining that can reproduce?"

"That's correct. You could be our only hope." I left the restaurant and walked back to my loft, stupefied by what I had just learned.

I was in hell, that's for sure. I was separated from my family forever. The digital phonebook showed no results for my brother or sister, which I supposed was a good thing. I couldn't begin to understand the situation. No one else seemed to know they were in hell. The human race was coming to an end, but if I was in hell then wouldn't that mean humans would no longer go to hell? I was in a state of confusion, and in my confusion I felt nostalgia. How dumb.

jimmy bean town

mired lara

THERE WAS ONCE A 15-YEAR-OLD named Tito Sullivan. He lived in a city that went by Jimmy Bean. This city seemed like everything was perfect. The people, the civilization, everything was perfect. Tito was tired of all the perfection and was on a mission to figure out how this was happening.

Tito lived in a world where everything was done for you. Every house worked by a command from whomever lived there. If you wanted an outfit, the house got it for you. Every building was like this. Jimmy Bean was a city where there was no way you could create a conflict. But everything that was perfect started off when you turned 16.

In Jimmy Bean, being a kid was the best time you'd ever have. Every child pulled pranks on teachers at school, and even though you got in trouble, it was all worth it. Every kid was placed together in one school, and lived there, just like a boarding school. The time you graduated, was the time when your whole life changed. You graduated at age 16, when you were ready for the operation.

The operation was what made you perfect. Before, you were an ordinary child who looked different from the other teenagers and the adults. This operation took all the imperfections from your body and made them perfect; you became amazingly beautiful. Everything about you was perfect, and you finally got to move out of the boarding school into the Jimmy Bean world. It was a party once you turned 16. You got to do whatever you wanted without getting in any trouble. But there was one problem; everyone was slow-minded in a way. It seemed like no one remembered their childhood. All they talked about was the present. Tito was 15, determined to figure out why everyone after 16 was slow-minded. He had a very short amount of time. This was where his mission started: Tito was in school one day, learning about the Jimmy Bean city's history. He had the curiosity of asking if there were any cities besides Jimmy Bean. He said, "Mr. Butch, I was sort of wondering about the other cities in this world. Are there any?" The teacher, Mr. Butch looked, at him with anger.

"No, Tito! There's nothing but emptiness beyond Jimmy Bean. We are the only living city in this world. The only working town with actual humans. So stop asking!" Tito just nodded and forgot about it. He decided to ask a different question.

"So, Mr. Butch, why are all the beautiful people in Jimmy Bean stupid? Well . . . that's what I've heard," said Tito.

Mr. Butch answered, "Who did you hear this ridiculous staff statement from?!"

Tito answered, "I ran into a 17-year-old, beautiful teen that I knew when he came here, and he didn't even know who I was! So I'm guessing he's stupid now that he lives in Jimmy Bean. Do you remember any of your childhood times, Mr. Butch?"

"Well, umm . . . let's change the subject, Tito. That's

enough Jimmy Bean talk for today." *Why did Mr. Butch not answer my question?* Tito kept wondering all day. After class, Tito was walking toward his room when he met up with his roommate, Chabela. They walked into the room, and got ready for bed.

Before going to bed, Tito asked Chabela, "Hey, what do you think about Jimmy Bean? Well, what do you think about the people there?"

"Do you really want to know what I think?" said Chabela. "I think after this operation that they all have had, they either turn really slow, or their memory fades away. I actually have a 20-year-old sister who I saw the other day at the park, and she didn't even say 'hi' to me. There's definitely something wrong."

"I agree," said Tito. "Why do you think they keep us all together until we're 16? We have to live in this place until turning into a beautiful, perfect person. Then we get to live wherever we want. It doesn't make any sense." Tito stayed quiet for a while. He laid his head down until something came to his mind, "My operation is next month. What do you think is going to happen to me?"

Chabela answered him saying, "I really don't know.

But we have to figure something out." They both nodded and went to sleep. Tito had a lot of thinking to do.

The next day, Tito woke up and was getting dressed for school. He was going to wait for Chabela, but he wanted to take the long way to see if he would run into any pretty teens from Jimmy Bean. Maybe he could get something out of them. Walking toward the English building, he saw a beautiful teen. Tito quickly stopped and asked, "Hey you! What's your name?"

"Me?" said the pretty teen. "My name is Poppy. Why? And why are you talking to me? Aren't you a boarding school student?"

"Yeah I am," said Tito. "But I was kind of wondering if I could ask you some questions. Aren't you Poppy, the one who would always pulled pranks on teachers when you were younger?"

Poppy said, "Umm, me? Pull pranks? I am way to beautiful and perfect to do that. There is no way I would ever do that."

"Are you freakin' serious, dude?" Tito said. "You're like a legend. I saw you walking and I knew you looked familiar. You're like 18, right?"

"Umm, yeah," Poppy said. "But I never pulled pranks.

I've been perfect and beautiful since I was born. What do you mean I'm a legend and that you remember me? How is this even possible if I've lived in Jimmy Bean my whole life?" Poppy was really confused. She shook her head and left. Tito couldn't believe it. How is it possible that a prankster like Poppy couldn't even remember the past—her past?

Tito ran to his English class and decided to wait until after school to see if he could find another pretty teen. His questions weren't all answered just yet. He was impatiently waiting for class to be over. Once the bell rang, he ran to the park and waited for a pretty teen to walk by. He saw a guy walking by the bench Tito was sitting on. Tito ran toward him and stopped the beautiful guy quickly before he left. "Hey, wait up!" Tito yelled. "Can I ask you something?"

"Sure, dude," said the pretty guy. "What's up?"

"What's it like at Jimmy Bean?" Tito asked. "What are the people like?"

"Well, Jimmy Bean is a city where basically we party all day; do whatever we want. All of the teens at least. The adults are either teaching here at the boarding school or security at Jimmy Bean," the pretty boy explained.

"Security? What's that for?", Tito asked.

"Basically they're there to make sure there's no students from boarding school coming to parties with us. At least that's what I've heard," he said.

Tito asked, "Do you remember ever being in a boarding school?"

"Not really," the pretty boy said. "Look dude, I have a party to go to so I'll catch you later."

"Wait!" Tito yelled. "One more question. Why do most teens walk through here?"

"Well, it's an easier way to cross town. It's when us teens brake our teleporting rings that makes us walk." The pretty boy walked away after saying that. Tito had remembered Mr. Butch saying something about teleporting rings. Since the students lived at the boarding school, there was nowhere they could go. They got their rings when getting the operation. So why couldn't the perfect people of Jimmy Bean remember their past? Why were the outside cities so protected? If there were any. Why weren't the students allowed in the Jimmy Bean town? Tito was determined to answer all of these questions, before his operation at least. He didn't want to end up like them. There had to be a way to stop this.

One day during history class, Tito noticed that there weren't any books relating the outside world. Mr. Butch never talked about it either. There was a picture Tito had found though, in the very back of the classroom, under stacks of Jimmy Bean newsletters. It was a picture of a car. No one had cars in Jimmy Bean town. So he asked Mr. Butch about it, "Hey Mr. Butch, what's this?"

"Where did you find that?", Mr. Butch said.

"Under all of those newsletters. What is it?"

"I don't know, Tito. Let me see it," Mr. Butch answered. "It looks like something ripped out of a fictional book. Just throw it away." Tito did as he was told but this wasn't something ripped out of a fictional book. It was an actual picture. After class, Tito had to figure it out. There were only two weeks left until his operation, and Tito still hadn't concluded or figured out anything. He had to work faster. There were hardly any pretty teens walking at the park anymore either. The only way to answer his questions was to sneak into Jimmy Bean town. When he was walking toward the English building, he had overheard a couple of pretty teens talking about a costume party next week. That would be the perfect time to blend in. All Tito had to do was wait.

It had been a week, and Tito had his costume all ready made up from scraps of his own clothes. He was going to be a prince. Tito had to blend in with the beautiful people, so he couldn't take an ugly costume. He also had to hide all of his imperfections from the security. The night of the party, Tito had told Chabela not to wait up. He told her that this was part of his mission. He put his costume in a backpack and sneaked out of the school. At the park, he quickly put his costume on behind a tree. Now he had to get by security. He was headed toward the Bean Building, where the Jimmy Bean citizens held all of their parties. With the costume, security didn't even realize he wasn't beautiful. This party was held once a year though, so this was his only chance.

Once Tito arrived at the party, he noticed everyone's costumes. They looked really beautiful and creative. He saw princesses, maids, superheroes, and more. As Tito walked through the first floor room, headed toward the bar, he noticed a teleporting ring sitting on the table. No wonder teens always lost these rings; they left them everywhere. Tito quickly took it and ran to the stairs where he was headed toward the second floor. He heard other teens communicating with the rings by speaking, so Tito thought of something. He said, "Take me to the operation room." Tito suddenly felt the ring shaking and in five seconds he was in a white room filled with operation beds. He had to quickly hide if he wanted to see an operation. Tito hid behind a bed and had enough room to watch. There was someone being operated on. He moved in closer with the bed to try to get a closer look. They were covering the student with a sheet over her whole body, and were taking her to go through a big machine. Once they had her in there, a big white flash went off and it seemed like it was doing something to the girl. She came out glowing with beauty. That machine had turned her beautiful. "One last step," said the operating doctors. They took a laser beam and pointed it toward her head. "No more student life," said the doctor. "Bye-bye-memory." That laser was erasing their memory to make them perfect! That's why there were never any conflicts in Jimmy Bean town—because everyone thought alike! All of a sudden Tito accidentally pushed the bed too far and knocked down two other beds. "What was that?" said the doctors, and looked over at him. The first thing Tito thought of was to run.

Tito ran and ran out of the building not knowing

where he was going, forgetting completely about the ring. He could hear security running after him, but Tito wasn't stopping. He ran and ran, it must have been miles. All of a sudden he couldn't see any part of Jimmy Bean anymore. He couldn't see the security anymore. All he saw was an empty road. Tito wondered where it lead, but didn't want anyone to know before they got rid of it. Maybe there were outside cites! All Tito could do now was teleport himself back to Jimmy Bean after he realized he still had his ring on, and that's what he did.

Once he arrived back to the town, over 20 security men spotted him. They took the him back to the boarding school, requesting for Tito's doors to be locked at night. Tito didn't care. He wasn't waiting until his sixteenth birthday when he would get operated on and couldn't go to an outside city. He was going to figure out this city's background.

A week passed by, and it was a day before Tito's birthday. He had told Chabela about how getting an operation brainwashed you into thinking that being beautiful and perfect was all that mattered. He told her about running away. She was actually planning to do the same on her birthday, which was in two months. All she had to do was wait.

Tito woke up before they could wake him up for the operation. He jumped out of the window that was the only thing not locked, which was on the first floor anyway. He started running the same direction as last time as fast as he could. But all of a sudden, a security guy jumped out in front of him and said, "Gotcha!" Tito struggled to get away, but more and more security guys ganged up on him. They teleported him to the operation room, and strapped him onto a bed. As much as Tito fought to get away, the doctors were ready to operate. They placed the sheet over him and ran him through the flashing machine that made him beautiful. The last thing that the doctors said was, "One last step." Tito was flashed with the laser and turned "perfect." His memory was erased.

cockroaches

grace maverick

SHE SAT IN THE MIDDLE OF THE ROOM, clutching her knees to her naked chest. She couldn't stop shaking. Her skin twitched, and muscles spasmed with faint memories of touch, the feel of the dank air pressing against her. She kept her eyes closed, for the shadows of the corners in the grimy, stained room taunted her, reminded her of the visions. She thought they were visions. She hoped they were. She hoped she was crazy, because that meant the rest of the world was okay. The room was empty, nowhere for them to hide, but she felt something brush her foot, and she held back a shriek, convulsing as her grasp of reality slipped away again.

She heard the sound of wings crackling, hard shells clicking against each other. *Exoskeletons*, the logical part of her brain told herself, but it was too late. She opened her eyes, watching in horror as the moldy splotches of the room started moving and turned into clusters of brown, inch-long shapes, with spiny legs and split backs. Soon there were more and more of them, climbing the walls like some grotesque ivy. She gasped for breath, claustrophobic and nauseated. Her skin stretched thinner and thinner across her ribs as she gulped for air; her sight became dim; her muscles were tense. The rational part of her brain that helped her cling to reality told her she hadn't eaten in days.

She awoke, staring up at the ceiling in a room so white, she was almost blinded—the complete opposite of her dark apartment. As all her senses came to life, she felt something covering her body and an acrid smell burned her nostrils. She shrieked with all of the strength she could muster, fueled by adrenaline. She flailed, throwing off the sheets, trying to claw at the thin gown that covered her stomach, but her wrists were bound to the metal bars on the sides of her bed.

She screamed again, tears pouring down her face—the textures, sensations, the new smells, the thing in her arm, all driving her crazy. She didn't know where she was or what had happened. In her room, she could tell herself facts; she knew things, but here, reality was different, and she didn't know how to find this reality. She kept screaming and screaming, even after people came in and tried to restrain her. Her voice was hoarse, but she didn't care, 'til someone jabbed her other arm, and everything went black again.

This time she woke up sore and aching, in the same room. Looking around lethargically, she noticed the needle in her arm again. *IV*, she named silently to herself. Sibyl Roy, the band around her wrist named her. The sun lit the room, shining through the barred windows. She smiled to herself, feeling warm and safe. The room was sparse, but not in the barren hostility of her apartment. It was clean, comfortable. The lights were bright and vanquished the shadows, but still, lines were fuzzy; nothing felt sharp or harsh.

The person sitting on the other bed smiled, hir (Sibyl couldn't decide if it was "his" or "her" face, so her brain settled on *hir* and *Ze*) face soft in the warm light. The room was empty of any personal touches such as flowers, photos, or books. Even the bed looked pristine, the sheets looked freshly starched, though there was a person on top of them. The roommate could have been any other patient, except for hir soft, wavy, golden locks, framing hir face like a halo. Sibyl couldn't quite decide what gender her roommate was, but there was an automatic attraction. All of hir seemed to glow, shifting in the gentle breeze. Sibyl opened her mouth, but her throat was dry and sore. The person stood and walked over, hir nondescript, standard-issue sweatsuit floated around hir as Ze poured ice from a pitcher into a cup on the table between them and held it to Sibyl's lips. She took it graciously, the crushed ice soothing her throat. She finished the cup and laid back down, but when she looked over, her golden-haired roommate had disappeared and a doctor walked in.

He said, "Hi there, Sibyl. I'm Doctor Weiss." He enunciated each word like he was talking to someone of diminished mental capacity. She squinted, trying to make out his face, but she could barely keep his white coat and pale skin from blending into the walls. He took a step closer.

"How are you feeling today?" Sibyl just stared. She didn't know what he wanted her to say; his condescending manner froze words in her throat. She looked over for some guidance, but her companion was gone. The doctor was talking again, but the words blended together, just like he faded into his surroundings.

She tried to concentrate, " . . . bad shape when you got here . . . gave you . . . Nurse Sophi . . . " but it was just white noise. She blinked, but she couldn't understand what was going on. She opened her mouth, and tried to ask about her situation, but it came out as hoarse gibberish. She tried again, but the doctor merely smiled and walked out. She looked around, but soon felt exhaustion claim her.

When she woke up, the florescent lights were brutal; noises were sharp. Her eyes darted around the room as an innate, primal fear over took her. The buzzing sounded like the flight of thousands of small insects; the click of hard-soled shoes on the tile became crackling shells. She writhed, squeezing her eyes shut against the vision, but her eyes flew open the second she heard the door open. She watched in horror as the nurses walked in, cockroaches covering them like some twisted fashion statement. She pulled against her bindings, fighting, trying to hide, as they came closer and closer. She squeezed her eyes shut again, 'til she felt a light, soothing touch on her arm. She looked up, and the nurses were gone, everything was swept away by the light of hir golden hair. She sighed, released tension flowing off her with a shiver as she relaxed against hir. The golden haired angel wrapped hir arms around Sibyl. The embrace was weightless, but reassuring nonetheless, as Sibyl fought to keep her eyes open. She felt the faint brush of lips against hers, soft against the sharp prick in the crook of her arm as she fell back into unconsciousness.

During the next few days, Sibyl was allowed access to the rest of her floor. She wasn't allowed downstairs to the cafeteria yet, because of her outbursts, so she spent most of her time wandering the halls, her medication keeping her lethargic. She saw little of her roommate, and the only thing that could bring her back from her trance-like state was a glimpse of golden locks. She ached for the sight of hir, but she could never catch more than the fleeting light of golden hair.

The only people she talked to were the barrage of shrinks, and even then, she didn't say much. She hadn't gotten any visitors: She had stopped talking to her family when she got a job as a financial analyst for a large business, stopped talking to her friends when she got one promotion after another. And now she didn't have a job. Her life, even her old life, was empty, and now, in this monochromatic facility, the only color she could find was her golden-haired roommate.

The next week, she was allowed downstairs. The instant she walked through the doors into cafeteria, the cacophony of noise overwhelmed her. The words hung over the crowd like some dark precipitation, bombarding her ears. She stepped into the line, picking words out of the air as she picked items from the counter. Turning to take her tray back to her room, the people pressed against her and rattled her sanity, 'til she saw a golden head in the midst of the dull flow. She pinpointed the exact table her savior sat at and quickly took the seat next to hir. Sibyl turned toward hir, basking in hir glow, feeling the bubble of sanity welcome hir.

"Help me . . . " Sibyl whispered, finding the words difficult to form. "I've missed you . . . "

Ze smiled, and warmth grew in Sibyl's chest, mirrored by the warmth in her cheeks. She felt embarrassed and awkward, but safe. Ze stood, and she followed. Ze nodded at her tray, then the door and she eagerly complied, hir reassuring smile never fading. She followed hir to their room, and they sat side by side on Sibyl's bed. She felt like an awkward schoolgirl as she scooted over to rest her head on her roommate's shoulder, golden hair soft beneath her cheek, as the golden-haired one wrapped her arm around Sibyl and laid her down gently on the bed. Sibyl closed her eyes, besieged with sleep, and when she opened them, Ze was gone.

The days went on, and she improved. She started returning to her former self, before her breakdown, before the roaches, and before her angel. She was returning to that strong, independent person, that cold, efficient person. She would always be strong, she told herself. She would not be weak. Not when she realized no one in her life truly cared for her. Not when she lost everything human to the job she dedicated herself to. She would not be weak. She would return to her job, forget this lapse. Forget being weak, and dependent. Forget letting someone in. Forget falling in love. She would be strong.

Her doctors beamed at her, so proud of her improvement. She was doing very well. She could leave very soon, everyone told her. She took her pills and told them exactly what they wanted to hear. She was glad to be gone from this mar in her planned, scheduled life. That's what she told herself when she lay in bed at night and her loneliness washed over her. She missed hir, and it hurt to admit it.

Tomorrow was her last day, or so the nurses told her. She curled up on her bed, clutching her knees, scared, but she didn't know why, scared to admit it. She was trembling, shaking so hard it hurt. She shrunk away from the feather-light brush of fingers along her arm, the warm glow of hir aura. She wasn't sure if she was more afraid if Ze was real or not. She looked up at hir, feeling her walls crumble all over again. Ze smiled, but there was a shadow of sadness in hir eyes, and she was reminded of her childhood, and the movie about labyrinths. "Remember, fair maiden, should you need us . . . Yes, should you need us for any reason at all . . . " She knew Ze would always be there for her, but Sibyl couldn't bring herself to finish the line, admit that she needed anyone.

"Well done, Sibyl," her doctor told her as he handed over the discharge papers for her to look over and sign. "It's not often a patient improves so quickly without a roommate." He beamed at her as she handed over the papers, now bearing her neat and perfect signature. She turned, and walked out the doors.

A roach scurried after her.

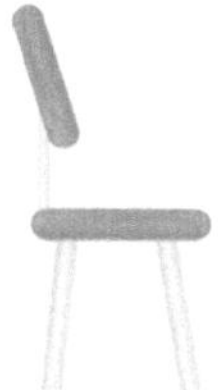

untitled

celeste pierce

CHARLIE SAT UP IN THE TREE, HER HEART racing, palms sweating, ears alert, eyes burning. Adrenalin pumped through her veins, pulsating through her mind, more than blood itself. Her heart was on a high-wire for more than three days now. Sleep scarcely overcame her eyes, leaving her just barely closing them, not even for a blink. Once, she thought, she did actually go to sleep, but the nightmare that caressed the night in her mind startled her, drenched in flop sweat and tangled in the hay.

Charlie resented ever choosing to be the gatherer. She

could've been the lookout to the barn, or the messenger! But she thought the gatherers would be much safer.

Sarah cooed, her velvet chest puffed out. They were coming. Soon. Charlie joined Sarah, her hands now wings and feet now razor-sharp talons. Charlie was gone, and a red falcon took her place.

Well, it wasn't her fault. All shapeshifters were to be gatherers. But if she knew what the "counselors" were to do after the campers got their wish, well! This story would never have begun.

The lights to the mess hall were over the horizon, for now the gleaming sun Charlie, Sarah, Rachel, and Georgina flew to. Their only hope was to survive Camp Willow. If Charlie ever got back, she would rip up the brochure and convince the government in some way to torch the entire place. But, this place was *set by the government*. An experiment. The government's scientists created a formula that allowed humans to become the creatures we read about today in fairytales. But they weren't sure if they could control them. So they set up three camps, just like Camp Willow, where they accepted the strongest, fastest, smartest, and most average college students across the globe so they could test out their weapons. Their weapons to kill just in case someone got out of hand. There used to be hundreds upon thousands of college students, some who could carry a brick but not realize its uses or some who could solve equations with just their minds but couldn't run fast enough to escape the clutches of the "counselors." Those all died. The Resistance now was stuck in Camp Willow's barn, waiting for an escape route out of the camp. The ones who joined the fight against the Resistance held the weapons, controlled the beasts the Resistance called dogs, and picked off one by one the college students who weren't good enough to stay alive. Some of the Cooperatives tried to rebel and kill the camp counselors. Only one, Richard, succeeded and lived. He killed off three of the Cooperatives and one of the camp counselors.

Darn it! Charlie thought, sending the message to the others.

What is it? Sarah flew beneath Charlie, looking for any Cooperatives or counselors.

Why did they have to get assassins and FBI agents to be our counselors?

It would be better than actual counselors, Rachel replied. *Those aren't as good. I'm not saying it's a good thing they got trained specialists, just saying it's smart.*

Be quiet! They're near! Georgina whispered.

Charlie dive bombed Sarah as she flittered away, squeaking. Rachel and Georgina were attacking each other, diving down to the ground where the Cooperatives and counselors were, their part of the play fooling them. The dogs barked and ran in the opposite direction, where the barn was. Rachel stage whispered curses and Georgina fell to the ground, her talons retracting and tiger's claws filling their place. Charlie swooped down and landed, her bare feet touching the wet, soft ground, Sarah following her.

"What is it?" Sarah asked once Rachel also touched the ground. Georgina's ears were perked up, listening intently to see if anyone was listening to them.

"They're headed to the barn." Rachel grabbed fistfuls of her hair and released them, her anger palpable in the air.

"Georgina, go and alert them. Sarah, you too. Rachel and I will continue on and get the supplies." The group split up, Charlie and Rachel continuing on skyward.

Charlie, Rachel's voice was scared but serious.

What is it?

I think there's a spy among us. Charlie's heartbeat quickened. *A spy?* Rachel continued, *I'm not the only one who thinks this. Everyone does. Except Michael. He always comes to the meetings but he leaves, sometimes, his guard. He never stays in the barn when the others are sleeping. Tell me that's not what a spy would do? Please?* Charlie couldn't speak. It *was* very suspicious.

Rachel, I'm so sorry. Michael was Rachel's boyfriend. They were together before they even came to the camp.

No. Charlie! Please! I know it's suspicious! I know that! But please! Michael would never do any of it!

But whenever he's gone one of our members dies. When they are on the hunt. He has to be the one. It just . . . never occurred to me. Rachel, if there was any other way you know I would find it.

You're not even trying to find another way!

Rachel, please. Be reasonable! Think about all he has done.

He has done more for the group than any one has ever done! You know that! For the first time, Charlie heard Rachel crying. It was very quiet, but her voice cracked and her sadness was coursing through Charlie as well.

The mess hall was now in their sight as Charlie came down; her cheetah paws tenderly caressing the soft sludge of ground. Rachel continued to circle the air, the lookout. Charlie entered the hall, the tables where she and her friends used to sit and laugh and throw food at each other. Now, where they used to sit, were several corpses, lying in grotesque forms. Charlie weaved around them, trying not to look at their faces, afraid that one of them might be a face she laughed with, one she hung out with. Charlie pawed the kitchen door open and saw Truence waiting there, her hands full of bags.

"You ready?" She asked as Charlie grabbed all the bags from her left hand. Charlie nodded and they were off.

Charlie was one of few who asked a specific wish. She could take anything from an animal and use it on her human body. Like the strength of an elephant and the speed of a cheetah. She could grow some tentacles and be able to take extra bags. And that's what she did.

Her feet thudded through the park-like clearing of the camp where she used to play flag football or extreme Frisbee. The basketball court was empty; basketballs lay untouched on the raised concrete floor. Truence's cursing worried Charlie.

"They heard us!" Charlie looked around. The woods were far away, but if she picked up Truence and combined their speed, she would be able to make it. Truence hopped onto one of Charlie's tentacles, climbed up to her neck, and held on tightly.

Charlie collapsed in the middle of the woods, the bags she held tumbling to the ground. Truence hopped up onto a tree and created bushes to hide her. Charlie's body glowed green with envy. She wished she chose an element she could control. She wished she chose the earth element, like Truence did.

"Charlie! Put the bags against the tree and, gosh darn it, hide!" Charlie ran to the foot of Truence's tree and flew to the very top of another tree, howling to the sky. Her horned ears picked up footsteps, but it was just one pair. Charlie swung from branch to branch, her small monkey eyes were barely able to make out a form from the branches. Charlie settled next to Truence and looked at her. Truence was concentrating deeply on the figure, and then gasped.

"It's Sarah! I think she's hurt!" Immediately, Truence unfurled the branches and swiftly swung down to Sarah's staggering body. Charlie gasped, but stayed hidden in the trees, watching out. She could barely make out what they were saying, and who was saying what.

"I . . . gone . . . "

"Shh . . . follow . . . up there . . . "

"They . . . think . . . "

"Do you . . . Charlie!" Charlie looked down to see Truence beckoning her to come down. Her feet this time thudded to the ground. She wasn't very good with transforming from a monkey gracefully.

"Charlie, Sarah, and Georgina were attacked! By some of the Cooperatives, Sarah thinks."

"I-I tried to get away with Georgina, but there were just too many! They just came at us! I was confused!"

"Did you alert the others?" The faint outline of Sarah's head nodded.

"We were on our way back to you two, thought you might need some help." Rachel swooped down and landed soundlessly next to the bags. She walked around and kept furiously moving her head, like she was looking for something. Or worse, someone.

"Where's Georgina?" Truence's silence and Sarah's hung head gave Charlie and Rachel the answer.

"What? Sarah, how could you?" Rachel exclaimed.

"I'm so sorry! Georgina came at them and I tried to keep her back but she just pushed me off. So I decided to attack the other Cooperatives but they kept coming.

It was so dark, I just ran, screaming to Georgina to follow but there was no response." Rachel was furious. Situations like this weren't her favorite. And with the whole accusing Michael of being a spy, it just made matters worse.

"Do you have the body?" Charlie asked. Sarah shook her head. Rachel swiveled around to the opening of the woods.

"Do you hear that?" Charlie's ears perked up. Barking. They were coming close.

"If we go that way we can make it to the barn and still be in the woods." Truence pointed to her right. Charlie took several bags as did the others and they set off, Rachel flying over the canopy, reporting continuously. Charlie swung once again from branch to branch, extra arms holding the bags. Sarah's back was covered in the bags and Truence held hers firmly in her fists as branches stretched out to assist her sprinting through the trees, only to shrink back once their job was done. They neared the barn and Rachel's sudden silence made them all worry.

Rachel! Charlie hissed, but no reply. Truence gave roll call. All were there. Except Rachel. Charlie's mind became frantic and she went to Truence, falling to the ground.

"We have to find her!" Truence hissed to Sarah.

"Come back! Rachel!" But there was no reply. Charlie morphed into a bird and raced through the trees, searching for Rachel.

I'm going to deliver the bags and get more searchers out here! Sarah thought. Charlie protested but Sarah kept going. Racing back through the trees, Charlie's eyes were sharp and hunting. Finally, she spotted Rachel by a tree and plunged down.

"Rachel?" Her body was facing away from Charlie in a strange manner.

"Rachel?" Charlie asked again, grabbing her shoulder.

"Rachel, honey—," at that moment, Charlie turned Rachel's body to her, then gasped and flinched away. Rachel had gashes torn through her arm and face, blood staining her hair and painting Charlie's hand a deep crimson. Her eyes were closed, untouched. The moment Charlie let go of her shoulder, she slumped down, her legs bending like they were broken. Charlie bent down to Rachel and numbly checked for a pulse. The thudding of a heart barely came to her fingertips. Footsteps came, rushed and scared. First one set, then more. Truence came and kneeled next to her body.

"She's alive, but barely. We need Henry—,"

"I'm here." Henry said, bending down to Rachel. His wish was to be a healer, but he could only heal people who were alive, even if it was just barely. He couldn't raise the dead. His hands glowed as they hovered over Rachel's body, going over every inch of her. Suddenly, Rachel gasped and starting squirming.

"No, no don't touch me, filth! Don't you dare touch me! I'll kill you all! I swear it! We will kill you all! You can never take my life. NOOOOO!"

"Rachel, calm down!" Charlie hushed, her hands pinning Rachel down. Rachel looked around then slumped back down.

"Oh my goodness I thought you were the counselors!" Her heavy breathing created puffs ascending into the air.

"We could tell," Charlie smiled, then hugged Rachel.

"What happened?" Sarah asked, pushing through the crowd.

"I don't know. I was just going through the woods when something jumped me." Rachel put her palm to her forehead and closed her eyes, thinking. Remembering.

"We need to get you back to the barn. Where are the bags?" Henry asked, helping Rachel stand up. Truence led some of the others in the direction she left them. Charlie helped Henry lead Rachel back to the barn. Sarah, Amy, Gregory, and Keith walking ahead, watching. Rachel leaned over to Charlie's ear.

"I have to tell you something. Something big." Charlie nodded and continued walking. They reached the barn and laid Rachel down in a bed of hay.

"I need to heal you some more, so sit tight." Henry's smile was more of a grimace than anything else. All the others were off to the side, talking and putting away the supplies. Charlie sat next to Rachel, her knees up to her chest and her hand holding Rachel's. Being healed was never fun. Charlie had it happen before and at first it was excruciating but then it got better at the end. Rachel's hand crushed Charlie's, but she bit back the tears that scratched at her eyes and nose. The lookouts went to the front of the barn, signaling the time for sleep. Everyone went to separate beds, but Charlie stayed with Rachel.

"I have to go pee." Rachel whispered in the break of morning, her voice echoing around the barn. They both got up, obeying one of the camp rules: always have a bathroom buddy. They talked to the guards then headed to the woods. When they were deep enough, Rachel grabbed Charlie's arm and swung her around.

"I know who attacked me," she whispered, incensed and pompous.

"Who?"

"Sarah." Charlie did a double take.

"Sarah? You sure you weren't seeing things?" Charlie could just barely make out Rachel bobbing her head.

"Sarah's the spy, not Michael! She's turning us against each other! Charlie, please! You have to believe me."

"Rachel, I know you don't want Michael to die—,"

"Gosh darn it, this isn't about Michael!" Rachel was close to screaming now, her hands grabbing chunks of hair. "Sarah attacked me, I know it! And I bet she set up all the other attacks. She probably even made some of the Cooperatives hurt her to help prove her story! No one leaves another behind. I was suspicious the minute she told me her story." Charlie shook her head.

"Rachel, I just don't know. It was dark; you may have been seeing things."

"I know a person when I see them. And I saw Sarah! When I was circling the mess hall I saw her walking perfectly fine, until she saw me. Then she started limping. Girl can act, I'll tell ya that!"

"Rachel—,"

"If the next words out of your mouth aren't 'I believe you,' then don't even bother!" Charlie's mouth stayed shut.

"Charlie, if you can't believe me, then who will? Everyone loves Sarah, that's why she's perfect for a spy! She has never firstly accused someone; she has never gone against code except with bringing back Georgina's body! She's the perfect fit. Put the pieces together, Charlie!" Charlie just shook her head again and started to walk back.

"At least tell me that you don't think I am a spy. Please?" Charlie stopped, turned to Rachel, and smiled.

"I would never think that. And if you want, I won't vote for Michael tomorrow." Rachel smiled and walked back with Charlie. They both flopped down on a sack and this night Charlie went right to sleep. The next morning, Charlie was the last to get up. Everyone was frantic. The girls were crossing their arms or biting their fingernails. The guys were silently arguing or walking around. Charlie sat up, confused. She looked to where

Rachel slept. Her bed was empty. Charlie bolted to her feet and hurried to where Tom was, one of the guards.

"Where's Rachel?" He shrugged, his eyes worried and his brow furrowed.

"I saw her come back with you, never saw her leave again. No one else came into the barn." An inside job, Charlie thought, then reminisced about her conversation with Rachel last night. She looked around again, this time for another person.

"Is it time?" Tom asked solemnly.

"I have a weird feeling about this one. Michael seemed so nice. Who would've thought that he would be a spy? Tory was the first to accuse and she said someone else told her about it, put the thought into her mind." Charlie shook her head.

"But who?"

"That's what I wanna know too." Tom said, crossing his arms.

"Are the Elders gone already?" Tom nodded, looking away, far off into the distance. His arms dropped to his sides, fear and anxiety apparent on his face.

"They're back." Charlie looked to where Tom's eyes

stared and felt her stomach clench and her head become foggy. She always hated it when the Elders came back from a killing; something in her mind never let the fact go. The Elder's heads were bowed and their steps were short, grave. Her boyfriend, John, was one of the Elders. He was the one who gave the sentence. John walked up to Charlie and hugged her, his face buried in her hair and shoulder while Charlie reached up to his torso, wrapping her arms around his waist and buried her face in his muscular chest.

"Are you all right?" He whispered as Tom walked away, his shift over.

"Yeah. How was it?"

"Grim. As always. Michael was such a good guy, you know?" John stepped back, wrapping his arm around Charlie's waist as they walked into the barn with the other Elders. Charlie's arm was wrapped around John's hips and they flopped down on a bed. Charlie placed her hand upon his chest and John rubbed her arm with his hand, holding the hand Charlie put on his chest.

"And now Rachel is gone. Do you have any clue as to where?" John shook his head.

"The others are discussing who should go out. You

and I were nominated." Charlie nodded and placed her head on the space between John's neck and chest.

"I'm just so scared, you know? I love Rachel. I almost went into hysterics when I found her."

"I understand. It's ok. We'll find her." Charlie nodded again, her fear, as usual, subsiding under John's touch. Jenny came up to the two.

"It's decided. You two, Sarah, Kenny, Tom and Richard. Tom and Richard will go out and find the Cooperatives base and see what they have there. Sarah and Kenny will sweep south of the creek. You two, sweep the north. The others will stay here." John and Charlie stood up, continuing to hold each other's hands.

John was a fire bender, his hand holding a small fire ball to illuminate the way just for them to see.

"I can't believe that just a few weeks ago we never expected any of this. And last week we got our powers! Feels like it has been years, not just mere days." Charlie nodded. They adapted most of the camp ways, like the Elders from the camp—really just people who have been to training—and the buddy system. If they didn't decide on what they would follow, they would all have been dead days before.

"Wait! I think I see something over there!" Charlie gasped, pointing to what she was talking about. John shone the light, but it was just a tree stump.

"Damn," John whispered, walking on while Charlie kept looking at the stump. She could've sworn a person was there. They continued searching, their feet sore and heavy. They reached the creek and sat down at the bank, their breath coming out in puffs. Charlie's nimble fox body swiftly flew to a tree's base, its roots curving out in some sort of bed. John extinguished the fire and lay there, Charlie curling up on his chest.

"I see something," John whispered, his heart beating beneath Charlie. She jumped off his chest and looked to where he was pointing. In the creek.

"You wait here. I'm going to go and check it out," Charlie said, standing up. She cut through the crisp, freezing waters, her fin moving the water, propelling her forward. She swam to the giant rock John pointed to and gasped as best a fish could. Rachel's head was on the rock, the water around it black. Her eyes were open and her mouth in a frozen scream. Charlie whipped around, planning on telling the news to John, but felt claws rip through her body. Pain burst through her pores and a silent screech was drowned by the water. The night grew darker and the pain slowly subsided. Final peace was slowly filling her body and Sarah's smile blackened her sight.

infinity

iris sosa

THE INFINITY SYMBOL IS ONE THAT WILL forever cause fascination in me.

I have observed its perfect, seemingly endless curves. The symbol for infinity that is universal is the lazy eight curve, also called luminescent. You know it's funny how this horizontal figure eight defies the laws of what is the beginning or the end! This is the reason I chose to write about it, and hey, it can help us come to terms with ourselves about life. What I am trying to say is that we should look at our own lives, through the infinity laws.

If we apply the infinity laws to our unique problems we just might have a better understanding of why good and bad things happen in our lives. Take the following saying, for example, "The old book is new to he who has not read it yet." A lot of times we may feel like we are done in life. You may feel like you've "been there or done that." Now if you look at it from the "infinity" point of view ,then somewhere along the line someone has not met you somewhere in the world. You may think that you have met many people in your life. But the real question is, have you caused an impact in them? You don't have to travel to a foreign country to meet people. If you want to know how, then all you have to do is turn to your left or to your right. The person sitting or standing close to you may be on the same curb in life. Often we go through rough times thinking that no one cares or understands our problems. The truth is someone else may be going through tougher times. So, you see, whenever you think you're alone in life, you're just not looking at the big picture.

a discourse on government

jeremy thompson

WHY ARE THERE SO MANY DIFFERENT types of government? Which one works? Which one is best for the people? In order that we, as a society, develop a government that is best for the people, we must first of all understand where we came from. What were the original reasons for government and how do those reasons relate to today?

Society, in general, began with the Creation. Whether by the Biblical creation or by happenstance is of no consequence; but rather that humanity met and interacted in the first place. This then led to some form of communication and cooperation. Current thought is that people began to come to understand the importance of protecting their property and life (Krueger). Throughout history it is seen that the strong prey upon the weak; and this phenomenon has recurrently led to the development of organized force used for the betterment and protection of the community as a whole. As time went on and these forces became larger, a need arose leading to the formation of the first government, whose sole purpose was to direct the organized force, or military. As David R. Krueger put it, "Government everywhere is simply that entity which controls the legal use of force," in which "legality" is determined by said government.

The intricacies of religion and government are extensive. Traditionally and historically, there have been three directions these two have gone: first, the coexistence and co-authority of religion and government in which both are equal; second, the religious government where the church or religion had all authority; and thirdly, the antireligious government where the government ruled independently and superiorly over the religion. Yet religion played a major part in the early governments. Ancient Mesopotamia, the Cradle of Civilization, is the home of Babylon and Assyria, and arguably, the first and most famous of ancient civilizations of which religion was a central point in their culture (Clark).

Religion was a major part of ancient societies. But to better understand them, and consequently ourselves, we must comprehend how they, and, naturally, we think. First we must understand that, we (humanity) are less intelligent and knowledgeable as individuals than as a community. We naturally and subconsciously take information that is gained from each other and use it as the basis for our own thoughts and ideas.

Alexis de Tocqueville, on his tour of America, observed many truths about America, and specifically democracy. In his book, *Democracy in America,* he observed,

> But obviously without such common belief no society can prosper; say, rather, no society can exist; for without ideas held in common there is no common action, and without common action there may still be men, but there is no social body. In order that a society should exist and, **a fortiori,*

***a fortiori - with greater reason or more convincing force; for certain**

> that a society should prosper, it is necessary that the minds of all the citizens should be rallied and held together by certain predominant ideas; and this cannot be the case unless each of them sometimes draws his opinions from the common source and consents to accept certain matters of belief already formed (Tocqueville p. 8).

What he is basically saying is that men (humanity) need each other in order to pool together collective ideas in order that a society should prosper. The collective mind is superior to the individual.

In their various opinions of government, many people were correct. Machiavelli was correct. Rousseau was correct. Jefferson was correct. But what were they correct about? Let me first tackle Machiavelli. *The Prince* was a brilliant piece of literature. His opening statement from *A World of Ideas* concludes his entire writing, "A prince, therefore, must not have any other object nor any other thought, nor must he take anything as his profession but war, its institutions, and its discipline" (p. 37). His entire position is that a prince, that is, the government leader, must rule with an iron thumb in order to maintain rule. Machiavelli is right in the aspect that the leader of the government must have military experience. It could be argued that the Civil War could have been directed better had Abraham Lincoln had more military experience than a few months in a state militia, in which he never saw combat. If Franklin D. Roosevelt had any kind of military service (of which he had plenty time before he contracted polio) World War II could have headed in a different direction had the United States not remained neutral. We (the United States) should have taken a position when it was obvious that we were going to have to become involved at some point. General Ulysses S. Grant was the General-in-Chief of the Union forces during the Civil War. He led the forces after a series of useless commanders who did not know what they were doing, afterward becoming the president of the United States. And look at Eisenhower. He was an excellent president and an excellent general. His military record speaks for itself and the fact that his presidential term was one of the most peaceful terms is astonishing.

Rousseau brings up points that need no real explanation. The *Internet Encyclopedia of Philosophy* summarizes Rousseau's main points about government: "Rousseau articulates three maxims which supply the basis for a politically virtuous state: (1) Follow the general will in every action; (2) Ensure that every particular will is in accordance with the general will; and (3) Public needs must be satisfied." As I previously stated, this excerpt needs no real explanation. The government should ensure that they are informed of the public's opinion, follow the public's opinion, and ensure that the public is taken care of.

Finally, there is Thomas Jefferson. As the author of the *Declaration of Independence*, he had the power to shape our country, which he did. His views and opinions are the basis for our rights today. The most famous phrase from the *Declaration* is as follows, "We hold these truths to be self-evident, that all men are created equal, that they are endowed by their Creator with certain unalienable Rights, that among these are Life, Liberty, and the pursuit of Happiness." Jefferson believed that every person ever born was born with rights natural to them and that it is the purpose of the government to protect those rights.

So, what is the purpose of government? The purpose of government as explained in this discourse is first and foremost to be a director determining the direction of an organized force as Machiavelli stated. Secondly, the purpose of government is to be the servants of the people as Rousseau stated. Where the government knows the needs and wants of the populous and caters them in the best interest of the country. And thirdly, the purpose of government is to be as simple as possible.

Take taxes for instance. Instead of a complicated system, which no one truly understands, there needs to be a fair tax on all hard goods, not on food, lest the government be accused of attempting to restrict the livelihood of the people, but a 20% tax on all hard-line goods is enough for the states to collect their taxes and for the government to collect the rest. The government should leave health care to the private sector. The majority of people can provide for their own livelihood and in turn health insurance, car insurance, and a home to live in. Although, in turn, if the private sector does not provide for the homeless, in which they try, but they just cannot do enough, then the government should provide for them. Instead of making it against the law to not have health insurance, it should be voluntary. That way no one is forced to do what they do not want to do.

The government should provide for the protection of

the people. First of all, the government should provide protection in the form of a militia in order to protect our country against foreign forces. Secondly, the government should provide a police force whose responsibility is to keep the peace and enforce the laws. And thirdly, the government should provide an intelligence service whose purpose is to collect information about foreign governments in an attempt to protect our country from external dangers, not to infiltrate into the lives of our own country's people, but to protect them.

In order to have a true democracy, all the people should have a say in the government. There should be a president who is the symbolic head of the country. There should be a supreme court as the head court, with other minor courts located around the country to handle minor cases. There should be a senate and a house of representatives modeled after the United States in which the senate has equal representation from each state and the house has representation proportional to the population of each state. There need to be town hall-type meetings monthly to provide a way for the common people to make suggestions for what they want. They can vote locally and then the representatives will be informed of their regions' position and vote accordingly. The senators will vote according to their conscience and then policy will be made.

In summary, a government of the people, for the people, and by the people is designed so that the people have all the control. The people make all the decisions. The people choose. The people protect. The people defend. Everything is the people's choice.

WORKS CITED

"a fortiori." *Merriam-Webster Online Dictionary*. 2009. Merriam-Webster Online. 9 September 2009. http://www.merriam-webster.com/dictionary/a fortiori.

Clark, Josh. "Why is Mesopotamia called the Cradle of Civilization?". 21 January 2008. HowStuffWorks.com. http://history.howstuffworks.com/asian-history/mesopotamia-cradle-of-civilization.htm 30 August 2009.

Krueger, David R. "The Origin of Government." 01 Aug. 2002. Web. 30 Aug. 2009. http://www.realitythinking.org/origin_of_govmt.htm

Machiavelli, Nicolo. "The Qualities of a Prince." A World of Ideas 7th edition. Jacobus, Lee. Boston: Bedford, 2006 35-50 "Rousseau, Jean-Jacques [*Internet Encyclopedia of Philosophy*]." UTM.edu. The University of Tennessee at Martin. 2006. Web. 30 Aug. 2009 http://www.utm.edu/research/iep/r/rousseau.htm.

de Tocqueville, Alexis. *Democracy in America*. Vol. 2. Penguin Putnam, 1945. Print.

music as a tradition

josh thompson

MUSIC IS SIMILAR TO TRADITION IN A way that's so remarkable. Tradition is passed on from generation to generation, it ne ver ends. Tradition is also a specific practice that has been in place for a long period of time. In the same way, music lives forever, evolving, adapting if you will. It changes, and in the midst of changing, it attracts people, fans in a way.

What do music and tradition mean to me? Well to me music is tradition. Music is literally my life. Music has changed my life and my generation, which will continue to change music throughout our lives. I believe that music will grow in such a way, and at such a remarkably fast rate, that it will surprise us all. I personally am extremely thankful that the tradition of music was born, constructed even, by people who wanted to give the hopeless hope. Who wanted to give the angry a way to vent peacefully.

Without this tradition I believe that people, generally, would be lost. So lost, that most of the famous events like: Austin City Limits, the Super Bowl Halftime Show, and famous buildings like the Sydney Opera House would not have been created. It is because of music and art that we have inspiration. Without inspiration we would not be so architecturally and technologically advanced as we are today.

Without inspiration I would not have been able to write this paper. So I think, strike that, I know for a fact that music is tradition. For it changes with time, and adapts to disasters. Whereas people would give up and surrender. Music is brave, and noble, it never gives up.

It also allows people an out for their emotions of love, anger, sadness, joy, friendship, etc. Music is the most special tradition to me (even more than Christmas), because it fits my every mood perfectly and passes my free time. That is how I illustrate that music and tradition are directly linked to one another with an incredible bond so unbreakable. Music plays a special part in a person's life, whether it is just a hobby, or it helps a person find himself/herself.

The first genre of music was, well, music. It was so long ago that it doesn't have a name. Music was first made public in the year 1204 by the Irish. By the way music was not invented, if that's what you're thinking, it has been with human beings ever since we were created. There are 23 general types of music. But there are subgenres that include specific types of music.

The music we listen to does not affect our behavior. It is through our attitude toward life that our behavior is constructed. I suggest to learn to love life and life will love you. My inspiration comes from a person whom I shall not name but is my dream. All my hopes and dreams come from my past. If you would do anything to go back and change, then why not use that desire to do anything to prevent the bad in the future.

Music has meaning, it has a purpose. That purpose is unknown right now but are we meant to know? Are we to be trusted with the answer? Will we be matured in time to realize that we are not meant to think only about ourselves and to be greedy with money or materialistic items? That is the question to ask ourselves. Do not answer with a yes or no because actions speak louder than words—prove that we are mature enough.

Why have these natural disasters happened to our planet? Well, maybe because the inhabitants have been cruel to this world. Maybe global warming is real and the ozone is depleting; maybe this really happening. Have we thought about that? When will we open our eyes and recognize?!

We need to think if we are smart enough to make music a tradition, then maybe we are smart enough to use music to make a message to the world to go green, or slow down pollution. Yeah, yeah, I know this is cheesy, "another environmentalist ranting and raving about his precious trees." But I'm not an environmentalist, I'm just a kid who sees what you don't want to see. I see a world of people who care more about their economy, and war, than about a common interest: EARTH! Why don't we put aside our hostilities and think about how we can work together to save our home?

The United Nations was created for a reason—why don't we use it? It's all common sense. Are we so proud that we don't want to be seen with enemies or that we don't want to be wrong? There is something wrong with that. Why do we do this to ourselves? It's hurting others too not just us.

Why were we cursed with these selfish minds, and why were we created with this free will, knowing that we would mess everything up? When will we learn that it's not the tree huggers who are stupid? We make fun of them just for a laugh when we should be listening to them. Factories and nuclear plants should be environmentally safe and not testing on animals. We should be helping not hurting!!! Hope for Haiti is good but not as important as pollution, because if we don't stop over-pollution then we will not have a home planet.

So, in conclusion I believe, without a doubt, music is another one of Earth's traditions that was made by the use of everyone with a heart and soul. I respect musical traditions, I am thankful for this gift. I hope that my generation will change music for the better, not for worse. With everyone there lies a dream, and with a dream comes inspiration. Inspiration is motivation, an idea in your head that you must use to fulfill your dream. I wish you luck.

the fox's funeral

amber tillman

THE FOX WAS DEAD. She was stunning in her beauty, mesmerizing, but still dead. She lay vibrant and still against glimmerless asphalt, her beauty marred only by the flies that had begun to accumulate around her face, to feed and mate among the caverns of her nostrils, and to lay eggs in the jelly of her eyes. But without the morbidness of that description, she was perfect. We had no idea what time death had claimed her, but even in the all-oppressive, dry heat of Texas, she hadn't begun to stink. She didn't seem dead at all, merely sleeping—if it wasn't for the absolute stillness of her breast, and the fact that she was lying on the side of the road, eyes open and fathomless, seeing nothing, not even seeing us standing over her, wondering how an animal known for its cunning nature was "outfoxed" (pardon the expression) by an automobile. Her body had not yet been subject to the eventual decay that all dead things inevitably feel (or don't feel), so we could barely believe that this animal, this beautiful and glorious, *wild,* animal was truly and completely dead. It wasn't proof enough.

Standing over her, the single thing I wanted to do was run my fingers across her tail. Just once. Just once, I wanted to feel the fur of the wildest, most beautiful and exotic creature I had ever met. I had never seen a fox before, at least not up close like this, and she was dead. What a meeting. A female fox in the prime of her life suddenly crushed beneath the wheel belonging to a car transporting human beings with their litters from point A to point B. I doubt the car noticed it was responsible for vehicular homicide. I doubt the humans driving the car noticed the fox at all, and if they did, I'm sure they didn't stop to wonder where she was going, or if she had children of her own. We wondered, standing clustered by the side of the road, picturesque in comparison to the oblivious cars zooming past.

I stood there, over her, my hand splayed in front of me as I considered giving this animal a last, loving caress. A symbol she'd never see to let her know that she was loved. A message she'd never read that thanked her for dying here on this street so elegantly. If she had been alive, I never would have gotten close enough to consider sliding my hand against glossy silken fur; I never would have gotten close enough to see her, if she hadn't been dead. I appreciated her death more than she would ever see and I had to touch her, just once, so she would know how much it meant to me. And I suppose she had been pondering too (not the fox), the whole time I was, because as I made my decision, and as my hand made its descent toward the auburn and white ending of this fox's ending, so did hers. We laughed out loud. How often are we referred to by the same name, or accused of sharing one brain inside two different bodies? How frequently are girls of two different parents, races, faces!, called twins? Anne spoke of kindred spirits long ago in her green gables, and the dark-haired Diana answered that calling.

Her hair matches the fox's pelt, mine matches the

glimmerless asphalt. Both our hands plummet toward the gossamer tail, our eyes looking straight down at the fox whose funeral we've come to attend. Eternity lingers, while we bend down to offer our condolences. Out of a blue Texas sky, high above us, two arms reach down. Clamp. Tight. A hand in each of his, one black, one white, but still the same hand.

"Don't touch it," he says as he imitates God. "It might have diseases." Our hands fall to our sides. We turn. Walk away. It occurs to neither of us that he is the diseased one, and we touched him all time. What did we catch, besides an all consuming hatred? What type of disease takes something beautiful and makes it foul?

And instantly, the funeral is over.

about the authors

madeline vuong

My name is Madeline Vuong. I've been an avid book-lover all my life! My mom used to have to walk behind me on the way to school to make sure I didn't get hit by cars since I was always reading a book and walking at the same time. My dream job would be to write novels, to write for *The New York Times*, or to write for *The New York Times Magazine*!

rey acosta

At an early age Rey fell in love with sports. He planned to try his best to make sure he had a career related to sports. However, he recently discovered his love for writing; at the moment, he is aiming to perfect his creative writing skills. His career plans have been left undecided due to his recent discovery.

samuel chapman

Sam is a native of Minnesota who lived in Wales before moving to Texas. He began writing in middle school and completed a novel entitled *Cold Snow*. His current project is a fantasy adventure set in a world inhabited by lobsters—it is better than it sounds. He plans to go to college and become a journalist and published novelist.

camille currey

Camille was a village child if there ever was one. When her grandmother used to take care of her she would always play "Scenario," a game in which you must invent a story. In a sense Camille has been creating things her whole life. She plans to go into publishing and help other authors' dreams come true.

olga garduño

I am the girl who's an immigrant, who came for a chance to succeed. I am the girl who plays the drum set, draws, and drinks coffee every morning. I am the girl who wants to follow her dreams, accomplish them, embrace them, and let them go.

sean kelner

Sean is a junior at SJDCHS and enjoys playing basketball and listening to music in his free time.

mired lara

My name is Mired Lara and I pretty much love to write. Not much of a reader, but when it comes to writing I can go on and on!

grace maverick

Grace has always been an avid reader of authors like Sharon Shinn and Neil Gaiman, so writing was just the natural progression. She hopes to one day live off her writing, but until then, she's going to school at St. Edward's University for a degree in psychology to become a therapist.

jeremy thompson

From a young age I really disliked writing; mainly the act of writing, but I still didn't like writing. As I grew up I only wrote when I had to, but I learned that I could write good papers. I wrote this paper for an English comp class and I found that I can really write well when I find an interesting aspect of a subject to write about. In the future I plan on continuing to write papers, even though I don't like writing, by finding something I like about the subject and writing about that.

josh thompson

I never really liked writing. Technically, I still don't. However, I do have a very intelligent mind, full of ideas that I feel people need to know. Also, I am surrounded by helpful, kind, and intellectual associates that inspire me constantly.

amber tillman

Writing has been my passion since I was a child. It is a significant part of my life and someday I hope to become a journalist.

celeste pierce

In third grade, Celeste decided that writing would be her profession. In sixth grade, one of her short stories got into her school's magazine. Her pieces usually have a darker side than what is in the text. Celeste's hobbies include classic literature, writing, acting, and hanging out with her friends.

iris sosa

When Iris was ten years old, she was inspired to write in her journal about her life and the things she saw in this world. She is now fourteen years old and still loves to read books and also write them. She enjoys being alone and thinking of a lot of things at once. Her favorite color is white, her favorite bird is a dove, and her favorite band is Simple Minds. Finally, her favorite writer is Stephen King; she loves his writing!

www.ingramcontent.com/pod-product-compliance
Lightning Source LLC
Chambersburg PA
CBHW030206130726
47898CB00012B/907

9780984189236